BRITISH RAILWAYS

PAST and PRESENT

No 41

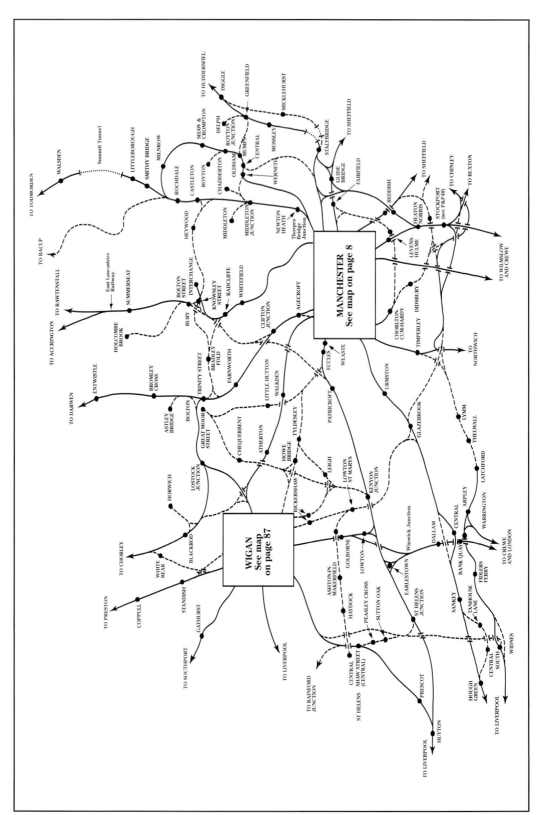

Map of the area covered by this book, showing the principal lines and locations featured in the photographs or mentioned in the text.

BRITISH RAILWAYS

PAST and PRESENT

No 41

Manchester and South Lancashire

Paul Shannon & John Hillmer

Past and Present

Past & Present Publishing Ltd

This book is dedicated to
the late H. C. Casserley

First published in 2003
Reprinted 2007

British Library Cataloguing in Publication Data

A catalogue record for this book is available from the British Library.

ISBN 978 1 85895 197 3

Past & Present Publishing Ltd
The Trundle
Ringstead Road
Great Addington
Kettering
Northants NN14 4BW

Tel/Fax: 01536 330588
email: sales@nostalgiacollection.com
Website: www.nostalgiacollection.com

Printed and bound in the Czech Republic

STALYBRIDGE: Looking eastwards from the west end of the up platform on 25 April 1951, on the left is the 9.50am Newcastle-Liverpool train, double-headed by 4-6-0 'Jubilees' Nos 45708 *Resolution* (allocated to Farnley Junction shed) and 45681 *Aboukir* (an Edge Hill engine). On the right is 2-6-4T No 42379 in the bay with the 2.30pm departure to Stockport.

The platform canopy has been removed completely on the up side, but there remains a bay at the west end used by local trains to Manchester Victoria. On 23 April 2003 Class 150 No 150149 calls with a westbound trans-Pennine service, while Class 56 No 56032 stands in the bay awaiting its next turn of duty, which will be returning empty styrene monomer bogie wagons to Immingham. *H. C. Casserley/JCH*

CONTENTS

LIVERPOOL ROAD was Manchester's first passenger terminus. Its opening in 1830 was marked by a visit by the Prime Minister, the Duke of Wellington, to Manchester, although he did not actually alight! In 1838 it was possible to travel through to London Euston from Liverpool Road, via Warrington and Birmingham. The station closed to passenger traffic in 1844, but it remained in use as a goods depot until 1975. After its final closure, the buildings were beautifully restored to become part of the Manchester Museum of Science & Technology. Our 'past' picture was taken just over 100 years ago in 1902. The nearest door has a notice over the entrance stating that it is the parcels receiving office. Several horse-drawn vehicles can be seen, and what appears to be a tar machine stands on the right.

The scene is remarkably unchanged today, as can be seen from the photograph taken on 28 March 2003.
Courtesy Manchester Central Library Archives & Local Studies/JCH

INTRODUCTION

By the beginning of the 20th century, the area we now know as Greater Manchester was crisscrossed by a dense network of railways, playing a vital part in the economy of the region with its coal mines, cotton mills and other industries. Much of the network was focused on Manchester itself, but there were also direct links between the industrial towns to the north and west of the city, including the West Coast Main Line, which gave Warrington and Wigan such a privileged position.

In the early 1950s, when many of the photographs in this album were taken, the railway system completed half a century earlier was still largely intact. But road transport was beginning to offer real competition for both passengers and freight, and within a few years the first significant round of line closures took place. Among the earliest candidates for pruning were duplicate routes such as the GCR branch to St Helens and the LNWR lines out of Bolton Great Moor Street, together with the short branches to Delph and Holcombe Brook.

The Beeching Report of 1963 hastened and intensified the process of rationalisation. Many loss-making lines and stations faced closure as British Railways tried to channel its resources into what was regarded as the core network – a sentiment ominously echoed some 40 years later by Transport Secretary Alistair Darling! Among the prominent casualties of the 1960s were two of Manchester's principal main-line stations – Exchange and Central. However, the impact of their closure was relatively small because most of the train services they handled could easily be diverted elsewhere: Victoria took over the services previously handled at Exchange, while Oxford Road and London Road (Piccadilly) took over the remaining local services that had used Central.

The closure of some secondary lines made a more significant impact. The large town of Leigh lost its only remaining rail service in 1969, while Bury was deprived of its connections to Bolton and Rochdale in 1970 and to Rawtenstall in 1972. And the cutbacks for freight were arguably more severe than those for passengers. By the 1970s the once intricate network of freight lines around Wigan was reduced to a single branch to Bickershaw, and between 1962 and 1968 virtually all station goods yards across the region were closed.

However, some lines on the Beeching 'hit list' are still in operation today. The Oldham loop managed to survive, as did the direct line from Manchester to Wigan via Atherton. And there have also been some additions to the railway network. The opening of the Windsor Link in Salford in 1988 provided at long last a direct route from the Earlestown and Bolton lines to Piccadilly, cutting out the bus ride across central Manchester for many passengers. The conversion of the Bury and Altrincham lines to Metrolink in 1992 was a welcome development, even though it was less ambitious than the 'Picc-Vic' tunnel proposal rejected in the 1970s, and Manchester Airport gained its own rail link in 1993.

Stations and signals feature prominently in this volume. In almost all cases the story is one of rationalisation, with many stations operating as unstaffed halts and many semaphore signals removed or replaced by colour lights. The group of pictures at Bolton shows how much change has taken place in just the last 20 years. Not that the modernisation process is yet complete: semaphores remain in use at various locations across the region, such as Atherton, Castleton and Prescot.

Changes on the motive power front have been dramatic. Until the 1950s the different pre-Grouping origins of many secondary lines were betrayed by their motive power, such as the elderly ex-GCR engines working from Glazebrook to Wigan and St Helens. The variety on the region's network at that time was huge. Nor was not restricted to steam. The Manchester area witnessed several early electrification schemes, reaching out to Bury and Holcombe Brook, Altrincham, and Sheffield via Woodhead.

The end of BR main-line steam in 1968 was undeniably a turning point, and its impending demise prompted photographers to record a number of the scenes reproduced in this volume. But even the diesels and electrics that replaced steam in the 1960s have now largely been replaced. Locomotive-hauled passenger trains have all but gone, and first-generation diesel and electric units have given way to second-generation stock.

The history of locomotive building is represented in this volume by a glimpse of Horwich Works, a facility that turned out nearly 2,000 locomotives in a 74-year period. The Manchester area had its fair quota of engine sheds, too. In the early 1960s there were 17 active sheds within the area covered in this book, together with a number of sub-sheds and stabling points. Today Newton Heath and Longsight are the only major traction depots in the area.

The selection of 'present' photographs reproduced in these pages presents a snapshot of the rail network in the Manchester area in the early 21st century. While many of the views look rather depressing compared with their 'past' counterparts, those of Manchester Piccadilly and Victoria show examples of regeneration, while the 'present' picture of Trafford Park shows the entrance to one of the busiest freight terminals in the North West – Trafford Park Euroterminal – now busy with domestic as well as Channel Tunnel traffic.

If the railway network of today is not quite what the planners of the 1970s and 1980s might have anticipated, any attempt to predict the next 20 years is dangerous. Among the likely developments are extensions of Metrolink to Oldham, Rochdale, Wythenshawe and Manchester Airport. No further extensions of 25kV main-line electrification are planned, but there will doubtless be further resignalling and track rationalisation schemes as and when funding permits.

On the motive power front, brand new 'Voyager' units are already ousting locomotive-hauled trains on Virgin Cross Country services, and 'Pendolinos' will soon promise a 2-hour journey time between London Euston and Manchester Piccadilly. The freight scene is likely to become even more dominated by members of Class 66, with fleets of varying sizes operated by all four of the country's rail freight companies – EWS, Freightliner, GB Railfreight and Direct Rail Services.

Finally, in a book that celebrates the past and puts it in a present-day context, the preservation movement deserves mention. The highly successful East Lancashire Railway is established between Bury and Rawtenstall and looking to extend to Heywood at the time of writing. With its impressive selection of diesels as well as steam engines, it offers a 'past and present' experience in itself.

We are grateful to all the photographers and copyright-holders who allowed us to use their material. Thanks are also due to Bryan Wilson, Richard Casserley and John Ward for their help with captions, and to Geraldine Hillmer for renovating and reprinting some of the older images.

John Hillmer, Wilmslow
Paul Shannon, Chester

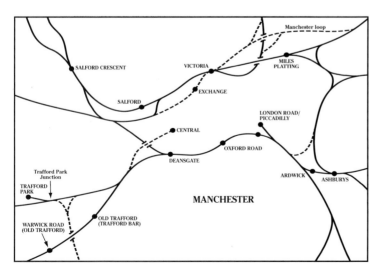

The railways of central Manchester

Manchester Exchange and approaches

Exchange station was opened by the LNWR in 1884. It was always closely associated with the L&YR's Victoria, and in the late 1920s the two stations were linked by the famous platform 11, which at 2,194 feet was once the longest platform in the UK. Technically Exchange lay on the Salford side of the River Irwell, and consisted of three through and three bay platforms. The imposing frontage was badly damaged by German bombers in 1940 and was never rebuilt. The station closed in 1969, 15 years short of its centenary. Services in later years included trains to Liverpool Lime Street, Windermere, Chester and North Wales. The GWR had running powers into the station and its locos appeared until the early years of the Second World War.

EXCHANGE (1): In this wonderful panoramic view of 1910, we see Oliver Cromwell's statue in the foreground, the wide approach to the imposing entrance to the station, and a line of open-top electric trams passing close by the cathedral.

Today's picture, taken from a lower level on 13 June 2003, shows that the approach is now part of an extensive car park. All the station buildings have gone and the statue has been removed to Wythenshawe Park. While trams have returned to other parts of the city, none pass the cathedral.
Courtesy Manchester Central Library Archives & Local Studies/JCH

EXCHANGE (2): In this view taken on 18 October 1946, looking along the famous long platform towards Victoria station, Class 5 4-6-0 No 5402 from Patricroft shed heads west, perhaps with a service to Liverpool Lime Street or Wigan North Western.

The footbridge has remained for use by Network Rail staff, but little else remains of the station. Most of it has been turned into a car park, as seen in 'present' photograph of 25 February 2003. *H. C. Casserley/JCH*

ECCLES: Opened by the Liverpool & Manchester Railway in 1830 on what became the principal LNWR line between the two cities, Eccles station has been in continuous operation for more than 172 years. On the opening day, when the unfortunate accident to William Huskisson occurred, he was taken to Eccles for treatment. Although described as a station, this was something of a misnomer in the early days as there were no platforms and probably no buildings. However, in this postcard view of about 1910, we see the fairly substantial entrance building, which includes a funeral directors, a chocolate and sweet shop and even the Station Cigar Store. Manchester Corporation tram No 25 awaits departure, showing Deansgate as its destination.

As we can see in the photograph taken on 25 February 2003, there is now only a prefab-type hut used as a booking office, open only at certain times. The remainder of the station forecourt is used as a car park. A plaque (*inset*) near the station entrance commemorates the facts that George Stephenson was the engineer of the line and that the Duke of Wellington performed the opening ceremony. *John Ryan collection/JCH(2)*

WEASTE: Until the mid-1990s the Lancashire Tar Distillers oil terminal at Weaste, which was reached by a short branch from Eccles station, received regular block trains of Phillips oil products from Port Clarence. There were no run-round facilities at Eccles and both incoming and outgoing trains were propelled along the branch. Four Manchester Ship Canal shunters were retained to shunt wagons into the terminal, and here MH24 and MH25 are positioning a rake of seven bogie tanks that have just arrived from Port Clarence on 28 August 1985.

The former oil terminal site was chosen for the new Blue Circle distribution depot for the Manchester area, replacing smaller terminals at Northenden and Widnes. It was built in nine months at a cost of £1 million, and received its first train on 10 July 2000. The contract for the new service was won by Freightliner, marking that company's entry to a new sector of the freight market. Modern safety regulations dictate that trains may no longer be propelled along the branch, so Railtrack installed a run-round loop at Eccles station. The 'present' photograph was taken on 17 February 2003. *Both PDS*

PATRICROFT was an important railway centre as, apart from the station, it had a marshalling yard and a substantial engine shed, which was opened by the LNWR in 1885. In our 'past' photograph taken in the mid-1960s, a 'Peak' approaches with a Liverpool Lime Street-bound express. To the left are the yards and loco shed.

Today all but the basic track has been swept away, including the footbridge from which the older picture was taken. However, with the aid of a stepladder we can see over the wall as Class 142 No 142003 forms a stopping service to Liverpool on 19 May 2003. *Keith Sanders/JCH*

Manchester Central and approaches

Central station was opened in 1880 by the Cheshire Lines Committee (CLC), replacing the temporary 1877 Manchester Free Trade Hall station nearby. The main architectural feature was undoubtedly the wonderful curved roof span. Following the 1923 grouping, the CLC survived as a separate entity, being jointly owned by the LMS and LNER. The three principal routes out of the station were the Midland line to Sheffield, Derby and London St Pancras, which came about after the Midland was given notice to quit London Road in 1875; the CLC line to Liverpool Central via Warrington Central; and the CLC line to Chester Northgate via Northwich. It was also possible to reach London via the GCR Woodhead route, and Harwich by means of the Liverpool 'boat train', which reversed at Central. During the 1960s there was a gradual decline in traffic and the final closure by British Railways came in May 1969. Being a listed building there was no question of the station being demolished, and during the period of uncertainty it was used as a car park. Finally a decision was made in 1983 to develop the site and three years later came the opening of the now well-established exhibition hall, known as the G-Mex Centre.

CENTRAL (1) This undated photograph is probably from around the turn of the 20th century, judging by the formal wear of the all-male pedestrians. A policeman stands looking at the photographer with an apparent air of suspicion. Underneath the words 'Cheshire Lines Committee' are 'Great Northern', 'Great Central' and probably 'Midland', which is obscured. To the left is an approaching 'balcony' tram – no other vehicle is to be seen.

Following closure the station was used as a car park, as seen in the second picture, taken in 1983.

Today we see how well the frontage has been adapted for the G-Mex exhibition hall, as photographed on 11 February 2003. In the hundred years or so between the first and third pictures, trams were abandoned but returned in the form of the very successful Metrolink system. *Lens of Sutton collection/Hugh Ballantyne/JCH*

CENTRAL (2): BR Standard 'Britannia' 4-6-2 No 70032 *Tennyson*, carrying a 9E (Trafford Park) shed plate, stands in front of the fine train shed. The date and service are unknown, but it must have been after 1951, when this class of engine was first introduced, and it is likely to have been a St Pancras train. At the side a Fowler 2-6-4T blows off steam.

The closest comparison today is from the Metrolink G-Mex platform, across the tramlines, photographed on 6 January 2003. This area at what is now the rear of the building is used by exhibitors for loading and unloading. *Keith Smith/JCH*

CENTRAL (3): Standing at platform 8, just outside the main span, on 21 August 1966 is ex-LNER 'A2' 4-6-2 *Blue Peter* (now preserved) at the head of 1T66, a six-coach special to Holyhead. The engine displays a 61B (Aberdeen Ferryhill) shed plate.

After the conversion to exhibition hall, the side of the building remained much the same, as seen in the photograph of 6 January 2003. *Gavin Morrison/JCH (with thanks to G-Mex)*

CENTRAL (4): At the 'throat' of the station, with the 1935 signal box on the left, this mid-1950s view shows a young enthusiast waiting for the next action.

The Metrolink G-Mex tram stop is adjacent to the old station, and in the 'present' picture, dated 6 January 2003, we can recognise at least two buildings on the skyline. *Courtesy Manchester Central Library Archives & Local Studies/JCH*

DIDSBURY station was just over half way between Manchester Central and Stockport Tiviot Dale. Opened in 1880, it lasted until the withdrawal of local services in January 1967. It was primarily a suburban station, serving a pleasant village that has retained something of its character to the present day. It was also served by a small number of express trains between Manchester Central and London St Pancras. Curiously the timetable for 1946 shows at least two morning London-bound trains stopping each day to pick up only, but no evening balancing services from the capital. The 'past' picture is believed to have been taken around 1895 and shows a pair of horse-drawn two-wheeled cabs and a single four-wheeler; the horses appear to be busy with their nosebag feeds. Situated close to Didsbury village centre, with the main road to Manchester passing in front, the station building shows a similarity in design with neighbouring Withington.

The line through Didsbury was axed in 1969, two years after the station closure. Now the only survivor is the clock, erected to the memory of local benefactor Dr J. Milson Rhodes JP. The old station buildings were demolished in 1981 and have been replaced by a small shopping precinct, as seen in the 'present' picture dated 7 April 2003. *Courtesy Manchester Central Library Archives & Local Studies/JCH*

TRAFFORD PARK JUNCTION was just west of United Football Ground station, and gave access to Trafford Park shed as well as to Trafford Park industrial estate and the Manchester Ship Canal Railway. Ex-GCR 'D10' 4-4-0 'Director' No 62651 *Purdon Viccars* (a Trafford Park engine), in the last few years of its life, passes the junction with a Liverpool-bound service on 13 June 1949.

Just over half a century later the railway infrastructure has changed completely. The junction has been remodelled and now gives access to Trafford Park Euroterminal, opened in 1994 as the Channel Tunnel intermodal railhead for North West England. EWS pilot loco 08954 waits between duties outside the Euroterminal on 17 February 2003. There is also a spur from here to the deep-sea container depot at Barton Dock Road, served by Freightliner. *H. C. Casserley/PDS*

TRAFFORD PARK SHED: Officially opened in 1895 by the CLC, Trafford Park had a brick-built 20-road dead-end shed. There were two turntables, water tanks and coal stages, initially for the separate use of the Midland Railway and the Great Central Railway, and later for Great Northern engines, as the CLC had none of its own. In the mid-1940s the LMS engines included 2-6-2Ts, 4-4-0 'Compounds', 4-6-0 'Jubilees' and 2-8-0 8Fs. On the LNER side there was a much larger allocation, which included ex-GCR 4-6-0s, 'D9' 4-4-0s, a variety of 'J10' and 'J39' 0-6-0s, together with 'C12' 4-4-2Ts, 'N5' 0-6-2Ts and a handful of 'J67' and 'J69' 0-6-0s. This photograph, taken in the mid-1960s, shows 8F 2-8-0 No 48273 and three 'Black Five' 4-6-0s, Nos 45188, 44815 and 44735. The latter carries a 9E shed plate, which was Trafford Park at the time.

The shed was reduced in size in the early 1950s and closed in 1968. The site was then redeveloped as Manchester's second Freightliner depot. The 'present' photograph of 25 May 2003 shows the entrance to the Freightliner terminal, with United's ground in the distance. *Keith Sanders/JCH*

Following the opening of Central station, the MS&L Railway (to become the Great Central) built a line from Fairfield on the London Road-Sheffield route to a junction with the Midland just south of Chorlton-cum-Hardy station, giving it access to the Manchester terminus. Never a busy line, it nonetheless saw a variety of interesting trains over the years. These included a direct King's Cross to Manchester Central via Sheffield service, which ran for a short period in the mid-1920s, a Marylebone to Manchester Central service, and a 'boat train' from Liverpool to Harwich. Towards the end of its life the line was mainly used by Freightliner traffic to and from Trafford Park. It was singled in 1971 and closed in 1988.

LEVENSHULME SOUTH: Opened in May 1892 as Levenshulme (GC), it was not until 1952 that it was re-named Levenshulme South to distinguish it from its LNWR neighbour. It closed to passengers in 1958, although the line was to last another 30 years as a useful freight by-pass for central Manchester. In the 'past' picture, looking west towards Chorlton in 1965, the platforms and station buildings are still in situ.
   Today the alignment of the trackbed is quite clear, and although the platforms have gone, parts of the station buildings remain. It is planned for the line to become part of the National Sustrans cycle network by 2005, running from Gorton to Old Trafford. The first 'present' photograph of 6 January 2003 shows work in progress for the cycleway, while the third view shows the surviving station entrance building on Stockport Road. *Courtesy Manchester Central Library Archives & Local Studies/JCH (2)*

REDDISH DEPOT was situated on a spur off the Fairfield line. It was opened in 1954, primarily to service and maintain the EM1 and EM2 electric locomotives for the Woodhead line and electric multiple-units for the Manchester to Glossop/Hadfield service. In addition, the depot carried out work on diesels such as Class 25s and Class 40s. On 15 March 1975 EM1 (Class 76) locos Nos 76023 and 76012 stand outside the depot with 'Hadfield' EMU car M59604M on the right. Class 40s Nos 40113 and 40119 were also 'on shed' on the same day.

The second photograph, taken on 2 September 1979, shows two Class 25s under repair, in addition to electric stock.

After closure in 1983 the depot was demolished and the area became wasteland, as seen in the photograph taken on 3 March 2003. *All JCH*

URMSTON: When first opened in 1873, Urmston station served little more than a village. In the 'past' picture, taken at the turn of the 20th century and looking west, the Manchester platform is crowded as a train approaches. The dress is very formal and the men's hats include at least one top-hat and a straw 'boater'. The railway official standing on the edge of the platform wears a peaked cap adorned with a considerable amount of 'scrambled egg'.

The station was modernised in the BR era. On 25 February 2003 Class 170 No 170506 rushes through with a Central Trains Liverpool Lime Street to Norwich service. While the station buildings on the Liverpool-bound platform remain, albeit not in railway use, those on the Manchester side were swept away completely and replaced by a modern structure. *Lens of Sutton collection/JCH*

GLAZEBROOK (1): Opened in 1873 by the CLC, Glazebrook station lay approximately one-third of the way from Manchester to Liverpool. In this photograph, taken just west of the station on Grand National Day in March 1939, ex-GCR 4-4-0 (LNER 'D6') No 5853 provides characteristic motive power for a Stockport Tiviot Dale to Liverpool train. The last 'D6' was withdrawn in 1948, just before nationalisation.

In the 'present' picture, taken on 31 March 2003, Class 150 No 150145 forms the 1227 from Liverpool Lime Street to Manchester Airport. The main line has become much more closed in by trees, but the house above the locomotive in the 'past' picture remains. *John F. Ward collection/JCH*

GLAZEBROOK (2): When the CLC line to Skelton Junction was diverted over the Manchester Ship Canal, its original alignment at the Glazebrook end was retained for access to various goods sidings. These included an oil terminal that remained in use until the 1980s, receiving block trains from refineries at Haverton Hill, Immingham and Waterston. On 4 April 1986 Class 37 No 37023 stands at the terminal after working 6M08, the 0150 from Haverton Hill. Traffic levels declined in the 1990s and the terminal took its last rail-borne delivery in September 1999. There is now no scheduled freight on the ex-CLC line west of Trafford Park.

On 31 March 2003 little remains of the terminal, although a corner of one of the gasholders can be seen peeping to the left of the trees. The vantage point for both photographs is the long-abandoned trackbed of the Glazebrook to Skelton Junction line. *PDS/JCH*

Manchester London Road (Piccadilly), Oxford Road and approaches

The Manchester & Birmingham Railway opened London Road station in 1842, replacing a smaller terminus at Travis Street. It was a joint venture with the Sheffield, Ashton-under-Lyne & Manchester Railway, but this agreement between the companies that were to become the LNWR and the GCR was at times far from amicable, resulting in the division of London Road station in 1859 by means of a barrier on the footbridge, a separation that was to persist until nationalisation in 1948. Meanwhile, the opening of the MSJ&A line to Altrincham gave London Road its useful through platforms on the south side. As the station prospered it became congested, and partial relief came in 1910 with the opening of the adjacent Mayfield station as an additional terminal for suburban services. In 1960, when the line to Crewe was electrified, London Road was renamed Piccadilly.

LONDON ROAD/PICCADILLY (1): Taken in about 1905, this view of the approach road shows a line of mixed motor (the nearest has the registration number N 7154) and horse-drawn cabs, making one wonder how the drivers got on together. On the left side of the building can just be seen the words 'Great Central Railway', with 'London and North Western Railway' on the right. The Great Western is not left out either, as it has a bank of posters just below the signals, which were in the London Road goods yard (LNWR).

   What a difference 100-plus years make! On 4 February 2003 the modern 'lazy S' building dominates the left-hand side, with shops at ground level and offices above. Then we see the new entrance to the station, while behind rises the office block occupied by Network Rail. At the time this photograph was taken, only buses and delivery lorries were using the approach road, a new entrance for taxis having been opened on the corner of Fairfield Street and Travis Street at a lower level. *Lens of Sutton collection/JCH*

LONDON ROAD/PICCADILLY (2): Our second picture, dated 11 March 1954, shows Midland Railway-design 0-6-0 No 44280 (a 10E Sutton Oak loco) coming off the Oxford Road line with a goods train, while on the right 'Black Five' 4-6-0 No 44686 (allocated to Longsight) is departing from the main station. No 44686, with its Caprotti valve-gear and double chimney, was one of the last two 'Black Fives' to be built, entering service in 1951.

Almost 50 years later, on 23 January 2003, the train sheds look much the same, but the platforms have been lengthened and considerable track alteration has taken place. From left to right we see two-car Class 158 unit No 158831 leaving for Cardiff, then a Virgin-operated Inter-City 125 unit, and finally a driving van trailer at the head of a Euston train with an electric loco at the rear. *John F. Ward collection/JCH*

LONDON ROAD/PICCADILLY (3): On the LNER side of the station, where the platforms had letters instead of numbers, two ex-GCR 4-4-2T 'C13' engines, Nos 7414 and 7424, are captured on film on 18 October 1946. A water column is behind the cab of the former and semaphore signals are still the norm. The two engines would have been allocated to Gorton shed and used on station duties and suburban services.

The station has undergone several rationalisation exercises and refurbishments, not least in readiness for the Commonwealth Games in 2002, when the main entrance and concourse were modernised. In the view of 25 February 2003, Class 158 No 158812 is on the left with a trans-Pennine service operated by Northern Spirit (Arriva Trains Northern), while First North Western 'Sprinter' No 150138 stands on the right awaiting departure to New Mills. *H. C. Casserley/JCH*

LONDON ROAD/PICCADILLY (4): Bearing the British Railways 'lion and wheel' emblem, EM1 electric loco No 26052 is pictured in 1960 after bringing in a train from Sheffield. Following the electrification of the Woodhead route over the Pennines in 1954, these services were shared by the EM1 'Tommies' (later to become Class 76) and EM2 'Electras'. The EM1s were also employed on coal trains from the Yorkshire coalfields to Lancashire and Merseyside, usually working as far as Dewsnap or Godley Junction, where they were replaced by steam or diesel traction.

Comparison with the photograph taken on 4 February 2003 does not show any great change. Today each platform carries its own monitor showing the details of the train at the platform, together with others showing the full list of departures. Class 323 No 323229 in First North Western livery awaits its next turn of duty. It is normal practice for two or even three trains to be in a platform together, which keeps passengers on their toes! *Michael Mensing/JCH*

LONDON ROAD/PICCADILLY (5): On 18 October 1946 LMS 2-6-4T No 2461 of Longsight shed awaits departure at the head of a suburban service, next to London Road No 3 signal box.

The signal box was closed in 1960 as part of the massive station remodelling and resignalling programme. There have been two significant changes in motive power since the date of the 'past' photograph: first the change from steam to electric and diesel locomotives, then the shift from locomotives of any sort to fixed-formation unit train operation, dispensing with the need for run-round movements and all their associated complications and costs. Typical of the latest breed is the new 'Voyager' Class 221 standing at Platform 5 on 26 July 2002 with a cross-country service. Banners for the Commonwealth Games in Manchester enhance the bright and clean appearance of the station, a far cry from the smoke-filled days of the 1940s. *H. C. Casserley/JCH*

OXFORD ROAD station was opened by the Manchester South Junction & Altrincham Railway in 1849, when the service to Altrincham commenced. It was later owned jointly by the LNWR and GCR. Although there were some through trains between Oxford Road and London Road, it was not until the 1890s that London Road became the regular terminus for Altrincham trains. The line to Altrincham was electrified on the 1500 volts DC overhead system in 1931 by the LMS. In the photograph of 4 August 1962, Ivatt 2-6-2T No 41213 is standing in the bay accessed from the Deansgate direction only, and the train is the 4.19pm 'push-pull' service to Ditton. At the far

end is the GCR-type signal box, which contained 40 levers, while the station buildings are those of the 1959/60 reconstruction – a distinctive style that still looks modern today.

The shift towards more through trains has enabled the closure of one of the west-facing bay platforms, while the other sees little use. The 'present' scene is dated 11 February 2003, with an interested station cat looking on!
Keith Smith/JCH

32

OLD TRAFFORD station opened in 1849 and lasted until 1991, when it temporarily closed while the line was converted to Metrolink. This view, taken around the turn of the 20th century, shows the station entrance with a characteristic four-wheel cab of the era. A lady walks past in a long skirt and elaborate hat, while the cabbie leans against the wall awaiting his next fare.

The station reopened in 1992 as Trafford Bar. The building remains intact and even the fancy metal adornment on the roof has survived, as photographed on 25 February 2003. However, the gas lighting has gone, and other signs of change include a modern telephone box, a bicycle, traffic lights and a car. The young lady waiting to cross the street is rather more casually dressed than her counterpart 100 ago. *Lens of Sutton collection/JCH*

WARWICK ROAD: The four-platform station at Warwick Road was a late addition to the railway network, not opening until 1931. Former GCR 4-4-2T 'C13' No 67433 passes through on 13 June 1949 with the 5.40pm Manchester Central to Chester train.

Warwick Road closed in 1991 for the Metrolink conversion project and reopened as Old Trafford in the following year. Italian-built tram No 1006 arrives on 25 February 2003 with a Manchester Piccadilly to Altrincham service. The station was reduced to two tracks in the BR era, and today the two remaining platforms have the standard raised sections to enable people with wheelchairs and pushchairs to board the trams. *H. C. Casserley/JCH*

ASHBURYS is the second station out of Manchester on the line to Guide Bridge and Hadfield. It opened in 1855 as Ashburys, changed to Ashburys for Openshaw, then to Ashburys for Belle Vue, and finally returned to the original name. In the photograph of 18 April 1954, ex-GCR 'C14' 4-4-2T is approaching the station with the 1.20pm (Sundays) service from London Road to Macclesfield Central. We can see the recently installed wires and gantries of the Woodhead line electrification, with colour light signals already in operation.

On 23 January 2003 three-car Class 158 unit No 158802 (allocated to Heaton) heads east with a trans-Pennine service. A Class 101 'heritage' DMU is disappearing towards Manchester. Note the tangle of razor wire preventing illegal entry on to the buildings on the left-hand side – sadly a sign of our times. *H. C. Casserley/JCH*

GUIDE BRIDGE lies just under 5 miles to the east of Manchester. The station was opened by the Sheffield, Ashton-under-Lyne & Manchester Railway in 1841 as Ashton & Hooley Hill, was renamed the following year to Ashton, and became Guide Bridge in 1845. Long before the rationalisation of the station and tracks, LNER 'K3' 2-6-0 No 202 (later to become British Railways No 61861) enters the station with the 12.30pm London Road-Sheffield Victoria train on 15 September 1945. Despite the fact that the engine had recently been in Doncaster Works, it was ailing and needed to take a pilot to continue its journey. The line to Stockport via Heaton Norris Junction runs off to the left. To the east of the station is the junction to Stalybridge and on to West Yorkshire, while the main line continues to Sheffield via Woodhead, not electrified until 1954.

While a shadow of its former self, Guide Bridge is still the junction of four railway routes. Our 'present' picture was taken on 23 January 2003 and shows the empty trackbed where two of the four tracks through Guide Bridge were removed in the 1980s. The Stockport line can just be seen on the left, with that to Manchester on the right-hand

side. Apart from the electric units to and from Hadfield/Glossop and the DMUs to Rose Hill, all of which stop, there are frequent trans-Pennine services passing through the station as well as a limited amount of freight. *H. C. Casserley/JCH*

Manchester Victoria and approaches

Victoria opened in 1844, with a single long platform used by both eastbound and westbound trains, and replaced the original Manchester & Leeds Railway terminus at Oldham Road. Traffic increased steadily from 1857, when Victoria had 58 daily departures, to 1882, when there were more than 250. In 1904 the station was enlarged to 17 platforms. In 1969 the neighbouring Exchange station was closed and its services diverted to Victoria. By the 1980s Victoria had become very run-down, particularly the terminal platforms at the east end. Salvation came in 1992 when Metrolink came into being, with the tram route from Altrincham and Manchester Piccadilly to Bury running through the streets until entering Victoria shortly after crossing Corporation Street. Also in the 1990s, the Manchester Arena was built above the north side of the station (opened in 1995), the track layout was severely rationalised to just four through platforms, and the station as a whole was modernised, though retaining its fine 19th-century façade and concourse.

VICTORIA (1): This view of the imposing façade to the station from Long Millgate was taken on 29 July 1966. The veranda displayed destinations from the station, mostly on the L&YR network, but Scotland, Ireland and Belgium were also included. Curiously the black cab scarcely looks outdated today.

In our 'present' picture the full length of the station frontage can be appreciated, as the building on the left has been demolished. The canopy detailing the various destinations remains, but the Lloyds Bank on the corner is no longer there. The accumulated grime has been cleaned off and the result is most attractive. The 'present' scene is dated 25 February 2003. *H. C. Casserley/JCH*

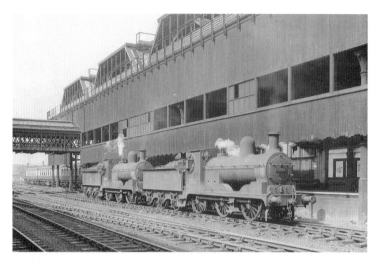

VICTORIA (2): One of the abiding memories of steam days is that of the bankers standing in the station, waiting their next call to assist a train up the bank to Miles Platting. In the photograph taken on 4 May 1956 ex-L&YR 0-6-0s Nos 52165 and 52271 wait patiently in the stabling siding.

The second picture shows an intermediate scene, with Class 31 No 31119 on banking duty and No 56095 heading east with an empty MGR on 1 August 1986.

Following the total modernisation of the station, today's view is unrecognisable as a Class 150 'Sprinter' unit awaits departure on 6 January 2003. There is no longer any need for bankers. *Gavin Morrison/JCH (2)*

VICTORIA (3): In the bay platforms at the east end of the station, ex-LMS 'Black Five' No 44851 shunts parcel vans on 9 March 1968, the year steam came to an end on British Railways.

While the station has been virtually rebuilt, at first glance there does not appear to have been such a big change at the terminal end. However, in addition to the remaining terminal platforms, a 'through' section was created to allow Metrolink trams to and from Bury to pass through the station. In our 'present' picture, dated 23 April 2003, Class 155 'Super Sprinter' No 155346 stands on the right with the 0848 to York, while on the left tram No 1008 leaves for Bury. *Roger Siviter/JCH*

VICTORIA WEST JUNCTION: 'Peak' No 45134 passes West Junction signal box as it enters Victoria station with the 0905 Liverpool Lime Street to Scarborough service on 30 August 1985. Within a few hundred yards to the west there were two further signal boxes, Irwell Bridge and Deal Street. The footbridge of Exchange station can be seen on the left of the box.

Following the complete re-modelling of Victoria, the closest view today is from the footbridge at the west end of the station. On 20 May 2003 Class 156 No 156464 leaves towards Salford, passing the site of Exchange station. Threlfalls brewery stands out on the skyline in both pictures. *PDS/JCH*

VICTORIA EAST JUNCTION: On 14 February 1989 Class 47 No 47193 *Lucinidae* comes off the Manchester loop with a rake of empty bogie tanks bound for Stanlow. On the extreme left can be seen part of Victoria East Junction signal box.

The 'present' picture clearly shows the position of the now closed loop line, to the right of the viaduct archways. The chimney in the 'vee' of the lines remains but it is hard to find surviving buildings on the skyline. The open space on the left is where the signal box was situated, while the lines on the right lead to Miles Platting. *PDS/JCH*

RED BANK CARRIAGE SIDINGS were situated north-east of Victoria station alongside the Manchester loop. Metropolitan-Vickers Co-Bo No D5707 is seen arriving with empty stock from Barrow in the mid-1960s.

Red Bank sidings closed in 1989, and the loop shortly afterwards. The area has now been allowed to grow wild. The link with the 'present' photograph taken on 7 May 2003 is the skyline with its chimneys and high-rise buildings. *Keith Sanders/JCH*

THORPES BRIDGE JUNCTION marked the eastern convergence of the two routes from Victoria (via Miles Platting and via the Manchester loop), as well as the junction for the Oldham loop. Curving round in the bottom right-hand corner in our 'past' view of 25 March 1981 is the Manchester loop, while in the centre right are the tracks leading to Skew Bridge sidings. Brewery Sidings signal box is on the left beyond the gantry with its six semaphore 'dollies'. However, also on the left can be seen signs of the future, with colour light signals. A Derby Class 108 DMU forming a Rochdale service, and comprising M51933 and M52058, is about to cross over and take the direct route via Castleton. These so-called 'power twin' units were useful for steeply graded routes such as Miles Platting bank.

The changes seen in the 'present' picture of 7 May 2003 are remarkable. The lines to Skew Bridge sidings and the Manchester loop closed in the 1990s, the semaphores and signal box have all gone and the permanent way now comprises just up and down lines with loops. The tall modern building remains on the left, but most of the others including the large industrial building on the right have been swept away. A Class 56 stands in the down loop waiting for a signal to proceed with a rake of empty vans returning from Knowsley to Immingham, while a Class 142 'Pacer' approaches with a local service. *PDS/JCH*

NEWTON HEATH DEPOT: Looking from Thorpes Bridge Junction in the opposite direction, the shed lies between the line to Rochdale via Castleton (extreme left) and the Oldham loop (off to the right). Opened in 1876 by the L&YR, the shed was a large brick-built structure of 24 roads, of which 23 were double-ended. There were two coaling stages, both with water tanks, and two 42-foot turntables. The shed was modified in 1935, and more drastic change came in 1959 when part of it was demolished to make way for a purpose-built diesel depot. The shed had an allocation of nearly 170 engines in 1950 and did not close to steam until 1968, the year of our 'past' photograph. The imminent demise of steam is only too evident, with just one engine on the extreme left accompanied by a range of diesel types including Classes 08, 25, 40 and 47.

Today Newton Heath is home to a large fleet of DMUs operated by First North Western, including Classes 142, 150, 153, 156 and 158. They are employed on a variety of services, including Manchester-Llandudno, Bidston-Wrexham, Manchester-Blackpool, Manchester-Southport, Manchester-Blackburn and Manchester-Oldham-Rochdale. The left side of the building has gone completely but the right side is basically the same.

The third photograph shows rebuilt 'Patriot' 4-6-0 No 45512 *Bunsen* standing on the east-end turntable on 7 December 1963. *Courtesy Manchester Central Library Archives & Local Studies/JCH/Gavin Morrison*

QUEENS ROAD: The original ex-L&YR electric units on the Bury line were replaced by BR-design stock (later Class 504) in 1959. On 28 April 1984 a Class 504 unit, comprising cars M77166 and M65445, passes Queens Road signal box with the 1345 Bury to Victoria service. The spur to the left in the foreground provided a connection with the Manchester loop and was used mainly for empty stock movements.

The Bury line closed as a 'heavy rail' route in 1991 and was converted to Metrolink. The box has gone and the third rail has been replaced by overhead wires, as a Metrolink tram heads towards Manchester on 14 May 2003. Whilst a junction remains, it now leads into the Metrolink depot. *PDS/JCH*

SALFORD GOODS, IRWELL STREET: This goods yard was situated close to Salford (Central) station, on the south side of the main line to Eccles. A pair of elderly L&YR engines, 'Pug' 0-4-0ST No 51230 on the left and 0-6-0ST No 51496 on the right, is pictured at the yard on 8 October 1957. The 'Pug' was necessary to negotiate the very tight curves.

The area has been completely redeveloped and the photograph dated 28 March 2003 shows a wide dual carriageway – Trinity Way – running beside the railway. However, the building above the arches still provides a link between the two pictures. *Jim Peden, courtesy John F. Ward/JCH*

SALFORD CRESCENT is a relatively new station, having opened in May 1987. Apart from serving the nearby Salford University and city area, it enables interchange between services from Victoria and Piccadilly. In the 'past' picture of 27 September 1986, platform construction is under way as a three-car Class 108/101 DMU passes by with the 1506 Blackburn-Manchester Victoria service. Windsor Bridge signal box is visible in the background.

Seventeen years later the island platform is a busy calling point for services on the Bolton and Wigan lines. Windsor Bridge signal box closed in 1989, and the remaining mechanical signal boxes in the area were replaced in 1998 by Manchester North Signalling Centre, located behind the metal fencing on the right. A Class 221 'Voyager' unit forms the 1205 Glasgow Central to Poole service on 23 April 2003. *PDS/JCH*

AGECROFT: On 10 December 1983 a Class 104 'power twin' DMU, comprising cars M53447 and M53480, rejoins the main line to Bolton at Agecroft Junction with the 0855 service from Manchester Victoria to Blackburn via Pendleton. In the background we see Agecroft Junction signal box, Agecroft power station and the closed Agecroft Colliery.

The spur from Pendleton (Brindle Heath Junction) to Agecroft was closed in 1987, and the complementary industries of coal-mining and power generation have long since gone from the area. On the left-hand side are the new buildings of the Agecroft industrial estate. Unfortunately, plans to build a Channel Tunnel rail freight terminal here were never realised. On 19 May 2003 a Class 175 operated by First North Western approaches the former junction with the 1215 from Windermere. *PDS/JCH*

CLIFTON JUNCTION: Opened in 1847 by the East Lancashire Railway (later L&YR), the station was renamed Clifton after it ceased to be a junction, following the closure of the line to Bury in 1968. In the view taken around 1900, looking south towards Manchester, the main line from Bolton is to the right, while on the top left are the platforms of the line from Bury, with a branch from the latter going underneath the main line before heading to Patricroft. The link to Patricroft was built with the intention of giving Bury an outlet to Merseyside via the Liverpool & Manchester Railway. Clifton Junction signal box can be seen at the end of the down main line platform, and on the low level line is Clifton & Kearsley Colliery box.

Today only the basic platforms on the main line remain. In the Summer 2003 timetable just one train a day in each direction serves the station. A Class 142 unit recedes towards Manchester on 19 May 2003. *B. C. Lane collection/JCH*

Oldham, Rochdale and Pennine routes

CHADDERTON GOODS: Branching off from the main line to Rochdale, north of Middleton Junction, was a freight-only spur to Chadderton coal depot. Class 31 No 31326 leaves the depot with eight empty HEA hoppers on 2 September 1985, forming the 7T85 trip working to Ashburys yard. The conveyor installation in the middle of the picture shows where the wagons were unloaded – roughly where the locomotive is positioned in the photograph.

The coal depot closed in the late 1980s following a long period of decline, but the area has not yet been redeveloped. The overgrown site is pictured on 23 April 2003. *PDS/JCH*

CASTLETON (1): Located on the direct line between Manchester and Rochdale, Castleton station was opened by the Manchester & Leeds Railway in 1839. South of the station, a triangular junction on the west side of the line gave access to Bury and Bolton. On 28 June 1960 L&YR Belpaire Class 'A' 0-6-0 No 52201 (a Bury engine), running tender first, is seen returning from the NCB sidings at Rochdale to Castleton. Platform heightening was evidently under way at the time.

The scene today has changed considerably, with the station facilities having been reduced to the 'bus stop'-type shelters. The industrial buildings nearby have gone, as has the signal box, but some semaphores remain, controlled from Castleton East Junction box a few hundred yards to the south. On 4 February 2003 First North Western 'Pacer' No 142005 stops with a local train to Manchester Victoria. *R. S. Greenwood/JCH*

CASTLETON (2): In a busy view overlooking Castleton East Junction box, Class 8F 2-8-0 No 48197 heads for Yorkshire with coal empties on 15 August 1967. On the right are the permanent way yard pilot locomotives, a Bolton Class 5 4-6-0 and the permanent way depot's 200hp diesel shunter. The loading dock in the foreground was shared by several scrap merchants.

Today the trackwork has been greatly simplified but the location continues to be an important centre for infrastructure traffic. On 2 September 2002 Class 66 No 66075 is leaving with 6E70, the 1201 Castleton-Doncaster, formed of nine YEA 'Perch' wagons. *Ian Holt/PDS*

ROCHDALE: The first station at Rochdale was opened by the M&L in 1839. It closed in 1889 when it was replaced by a second station a quarter of a mile to the north. This was substantial, consisting of two island platforms with two bays at the north end of the down platforms and the south end of the up (Manchester Victoria direct) platforms. On the Yorkshire side of the station, the Oldham loop diverged to the east. On 29 March 1976 Class 47 Brush Type 4 No 47530 passes the station with a train of empty coal wagons returning to Yorkshire.

The station and trackwork have been rationalised and the up island platform taken out of use, leaving the down island, with a single-track bay at the east end, to handle trains in both directions, as seen in the 'present' picture of 4 February 2003. Although the signal box remains, all the semaphore signals have been replaced by colour lights. The 'feather' on the left-hand signal (RE 3) is for trains taking the Oldham line. Looking into the not too distant future, the Manchester/Rochdale/Oldham lines are expected to become part of the Metrolink tram system. *David Flitcroft/JCH*

SMITHY BRIDGE is the next station north of Rochdale on the line to Todmorden. It was opened in 1839 by the Manchester & Leeds Railway and closed in 1960, but was to re-open in 1985. Just prior to closure, on 5 April 1959, we see the view looking north-east towards Littleborough. The wheel controlling the crossing gates is visible inside the box, and beyond the crossing lies the down platform. On the left can be seen the end of a long loop rejoining the eastbound track just before the road crossing.

During reconstruction the original down platform north of the crossing was replaced by a new one on the south side, opposite the up platform. The gates have given way to barriers, the semaphores and loop have gone, but the signal box remains, as seen in the rather wintry scene of 4 February 2003. At the time of writing the line sees a half-hourly service between Manchester and either Selby or York. *Gavin Morrison/JCH*

LITTLEBOROUGH is the last station on the line out of Manchester to come within the Manchester Passenger Transport Executive area. It was built by the Manchester & Leeds Railway, later to become part of the Lancashire & Yorkshire Railway, and opened in 1839. Bearing the 'lion and wheel' emblem, English Electric Type 3 No D6806 passes through with the 1X21 Doncaster to Blackpool excursion on 28 July 1963. This is believed to have been the first sighting of an English Electric Type 3 in the Rochdale area.

The 'present' picture, taken on 11 February 2003, shows considerable change. The original up (Manchester-bound) island platform has been replaced by a single face, further west, so that the platforms are now staggered. The semaphore signals have gone, but the down-side platform and station building appear to be mostly unchanged. Class 158 No 158750 forms the 1148 service from Manchester Victoria to York. Adjacent to the station on the town side is a small bus interchange area, named 'George Stephenson Square' to commemorate the engineer who planned the line. *R. S. Greenwood/ JCH*

SUMMIT: Just after emerging from the south end of Summit Tunnel, Caprotti Class 5 4-6-0 No 44755 of Edgeley shed heads towards Rochdale with a mixed goods train on 25 September 1962. This was long before the days of Preston power box, which for historical BR 'divisional' reasons was to take over this stretch of L&YR main line between Smithy Bridge and Hebden Bridge in the 1970s. In the left distance a Rochdale Corporation Transport double-decker makes its way back to Rochdale from Littleborough Summit terminus.

Comparison with the 'present' picture taken on 8 April 2003 shows little change, as 'Sprinter' No 150275 (Neville Hill) passes with a Selby-Manchester Victoria service. The semaphore signals have gone and the nearest signal box is 2 miles away at Smithy Bridge. *Ian Holt/JCH*

WALSDEN, prior to 1888, was in Lancashire, but boundary changes transferred it to West Yorkshire. A board outside the station provides a potted history of the town and hints rather broadly that there is considerable local sympathy towards the Red Rose county – hence the inclusion in this book. The first station opened in 1845 and lasted well over 100 years until closure in 1961. In the final year of steam, 'Britannia' 4-6-2 No 70013 *Oliver Cromwell* heads west with the 1T85 'special' on 28 April 1968. At the time Walsden had a level crossing, crossover and signal box.

In the photograph taken on 8 April 2003 none of those railway features remains, but Walsden Junior School is still there! However, in 1990 Walsden acquired a new station on a site just south of the old one, behind the 1968 photographer. Arriva Trains North Class 158 unit No 158762 calls with a Manchester Victoria to York service. *Gavin Morrison/JCH*

The Oldham loop leaves the Victoria to Castleton line at Thorpes Bridge Junction and rejoins it just east of Rochdale at Rochdale Junction. There are currently nine intermediate stations, Derker being the most recent addition, having opened in 1985. Following the success of the Manchester Metrolink tram operation, the Government gave financial approval in 2000 to convert the loop line to tramway operation, with new alignments servicing the town centres of Oldham and Rochdale, but work is not expected to start until May 2004 at the earliest.

OLDHAM MUMPS was opened in 1847 by the Manchester & Leeds Railway, later L&YR, on the line that was ultimately to be known as the 'Oldham loop'. On 23 May 1979 a DMU leaves the station forming the 1700 Manchester Victoria to Manchester Victoria service, out via Rochdale and returning via Oldham. The extensive goods yard was still busy with van traffic in the 1970s.

The station has since been reduced to an island platform, while most of the surrounding mills have been demolished and replaced by modern buildings, and the line has become much more enclosed by trees. On 18 February 2003 Class 142 'Pacer' No 142043 approaches the station with a Victoria to Rochdale service. *Tom Heavyside/JCH*

ROYTON station lay at the end of a short branch from the Oldham-Rochdale line. It opened to passengers in 1864 and remained in operation until 1966, with just a short break in service from 1916 to 1919. The single platform could hold up to eight coaches. On 18 July 1955 BR Standard 2-6-4T No 80052 stands at the head of a service to Manchester Victoria. On the right-hand side is the goods yard, which was to close two years before the end of passenger services.

Today the area has been completely redeveloped as a housing estate and the only link with the 'present' picture is the top of the clock tower of Royton town hall, which can just be seen between the two buildings, photographed on 23 May 2003. The branch is also remembered by a pub called 'The Railway' close to where the station was situated. *T. J. Edgington/JCH*

SHAW & CROMPTON was opened by the L&YR as Shaw in 1863 and renamed to the existing title in 1897. On 20 June 1964 'Britannia' Class 4-6-2 No 70045 *Lord Rowallan* enters the station with a Shaw to Blackpool excursion, a scheduled weekend train in connection with Oldham area 'Wakes' holidays.

The line between Shaw and Rochdale was singled in 1980. In the 'present' photograph of 18 February 2003, the warehouses to the left with attendant sidings have gone, replaced by a modern housing estate. 'Pacer' 142055 forms the 1356 service from Rochdale to Kirby, these units being the mainstay of the line. A second one can be seen on the left, having terminated at Shaw and now about to run back into the station to form the 1417 to Wigan Wallgate. At certain periods of the day there are four trains an hour from Shaw to Victoria. *Ian Holt/JCH*

MILNROW station also opened in 1863. Looking north towards the station, Horwich-built 'Crab' 2-6-0 No 42721 (which was an Agecroft-allocated engine for a long period until March 1957) trundles towards New Hey on 26 May 1961 with a short goods train from Preston to Royton Junction. The consist includes an ex-GWR brake-van.

Today the scene is remarkably different. The photograph of 8 April 2003 shows the line now singled (between Rochdale and Shaw), a road by-pass between the track and the houses on the left, a new housing estate on the right, and the station simplified to a single platform. At least the hills on the skyline remain the same! 'Pacer' Class 142 No 142023 forms the 0826 Rochdale to Southport service. *R. S. Greenwood/JCH*

LEES: This LNWR station opened in 1856 and closed in 1955, just one year short of its centenary. The photograph, taken on 19 April 1954 and looking towards Greenfield, shows the rather run-down platforms. The line off to the right led into the goods shed.

Other than the alignment of the track, nothing remains and the area has been transformed into a housing estate and pleasant walkway, as seen on 23 May 2003. *H. C. Casserley/JCH*

STALYBRIDGE (1): Formerly in Cheshire, Stalybridge became part of Greater Manchester in 1974. The main station was opened in 1845 by the Stalybridge, Ashton-under-Lyne & Manchester Railway. A second station in the town was operated by the L&YR from 1846 until 1849, and again from 1869 until 1917. By 1849 the main station was handling LNWR trains over the Pennines between Liverpool and Leeds, and soon proved inadequate; in 1885 a new and improved facility came into use on the same site. In the first picture, taken on 25 April 1951 and looking east, the station signal box straddles the main platforms and centre through roads. In 1893 there were five boxes in the station area.

Comparison with the photograph taken on 23 April 2003 shows how much rationalisation has taken place, leaving the station with the up (westbound) and down platform lines together with an up bay at the west end. Only one signal box remains, at the Manchester end of the station. Class 158 No 158811 heads for Piccadilly with a trans-Pennine service operated by Arriva Trains Northern. *H. C. Casserley/JCH*

STALYBRIDGE (2): A short distance from the station, towards Huddersfield, the line enters Stalybridge Tunnel. At one time this was the start of the loop line that ran via Micklehurst to Diggle. On 27 April 1968, shortly before the end of steam, BR Standard 5MT 4-6-0 No 73050 pilots sister locomotive No 73069 with an eastbound 'special', showing reporting number 1Z77; both locomotives were allocated to Patricroft shed. The freight line on the left bypasses the station platforms.

Apart from the obvious removal of the Micklehurst line, the overall scene has not changed very much in the 30-odd years to 8 April 2003, when the 'present' picture was taken. But whereas at one time the cross-Pennine trains were formed of ten coaches or more, today the norm is a two- or three-car diesel unit. Here No 158804 forms a Liverpool-Newcastle service. *Gavin Morrison/JCH*

ROUGHTOWN: Just to the north of Mossley station, looking north-east along the valley towards Greenfield, this undated view of Mossley coal yard shows a concentration of four-wheel wagons. Mossley No 2 box is on the left. Note the yard crane by the end of the terrace, and how close one chimney is to the up main! There are nine chimney stacks to be seen, but only one shows any smoke, which makes one wonder whether the photograph was taken during a 'Wakes Week'. The only road transport is a horse and cart on the road between the two chimneys on the left. Running along the hillside behind the mills is the Micklehurst loop.

Today, as photographed on 8 April 2003, the sidings have gone, as has the signal box, and a single chimney remains by the mill in the centre. A three-car Class 158 unit heads towards Yorkshire with a trans-Pennine service. *John Ryan collection/JCH*

DELPH: The Delph branch left the main Stalybridge-Huddersfield line three-quarters of a mile north of Greenfield. It opened in 1851 and retained a passenger service until 1955, four years beyond its centenary. The use of a single horse-drawn coach in the early days of branch operation brought about the nickname 'Delph Donkey', which was retained in the steam era. On 19 April 1954 Fowler 2-6-2T No 40059 has just arrived with the 5.22pm departure from Oldham. The two coaches are Nos 3425 and 3419, both ex-LNWR vehicles.

The branch closed to goods in 1963 and the track was lifted soon afterwards. The station building has since been turned into a private house, as photographed on 8 April 2003. The platform can just be seen between the branches of the tree in the foreground. *H. C. Casserley/JCH*

Bury

BURY KNOWSLEY STREET lay on the east-west route that once connected the cotton towns of Rochdale, Bury and Bolton. This route was opened by the L&YR in 1848 and remained in use for passenger traffic until 1970. 'Black Five' 4-6-0 No 44743 enters Knowsley Street on 2 March 1963 with the 9.5am Liverpool Exchange to Rochdale express. The tracks curving off to the right behind the train provided a connection with the electric line to Bury Bolton Street, used mainly by freight.

The section from Bury Knowsley Street to Bolton closed completely in 1970, but the remainder of the line, including the Bolton Street curve, remained open for coal trains to Rawtenstall until December 1980. Fortunately the station area escaped redevelopment in the 1980s and the track was later re-instated for the proposed – and subsequently much delayed – extension of the preserved East Lancashire Railway from Bury to Heywood. The 'present' photograph is dated 15 March 2003. *R. S. Greenwood/PDS*

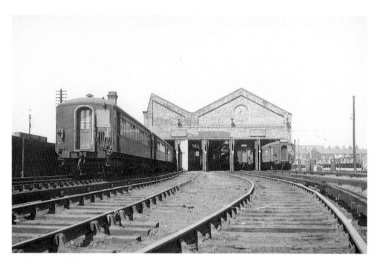

BURY ELECTRIC DEPOT: The L&YR was a pioneer of railway electrification. Its successes in the Liverpool area led it to electrify two lines in the Bury area in the early 20th century: the Holcombe Brook branch in 1913 and the Manchester-Whitefield-Bury line in 1916. The trains were remarkably modern for their time, with central gangways and end doors enabling easy movement between the coaches, and not until the late 1950s were replacements considered necessary. A gathering of first-generation stock is pictured at Buckley Wells depot, just south of Bury Bolton Street, in the spring of 1959.

The same depot, though with some structural alterations, was home to the BR Class 504 electric units that replaced the L&YR stock in 1959. Although the new units were based on a standard BR design, the electrification system of 1,200 volts DC with a side-contact third rail made them unique, and they could not operate anywhere else. Cars M65449, M77170 and M77165 are stabled outside the shed on 20 July 1990.

The conversion of the Bury line to Metrolink made the Class 504 units redundant. The depot meanwhile became a useful maintenance base for the East Lancashire Railway. Among the residents pictured on 15 March 2003 are Class 08 shunters 08780 and 08479. *J. B. Horne (courtesy John F. Ward)/PDS (2)*

BURY BOLTON STREET (1): The railway age reached Bury in 1846 with the opening of the line from Clifton Junction to Rawtenstall by the East Lancashire Railway. The ELR soon became part of the L&YR, a fact proudly proclaimed in this early-20th-century postcard of Bury Bolton Street station.

The upper concourse buildings, including the former ELR headquarters, were destroyed by fire in 1952 and replaced by a more utilitarian structure. In 1980 BR train services were transferred to Bury Interchange, allowing the East Lancashire Railway preservation group to adopt Bolton Street as its headquarters and southern terminus. The present frontage is pictured on 7 May 2003. *John Ryan collection/JCH*

BURY BOLTON STREET (2): Two Class 504 electric units await their next duty at Bury Bolton Street in this late 1970s scene. The station buildings look to be in reasonably good condition, but the track layout has already been rationalised with just one line continuing as a through route for coal trains to Rawtenstall.

Nearly 20 years later the double-track formation through the station has been restored for use by the East Lancashire Railway. Electric traction has given way to steam and diesel, with a far greater variety of motive power than would have been seen in LMS or BR days. Class 40 No 40135 arrives at Bolton Street with a morning train from Rawtenstall on 15 March 2003. This locomotive is one of two Class 40s based on the East Lancashire Railway; it was withdrawn from BR stock in 1986 and acquired by the Class Forty Preservation Society in 1988. Other diesel types that can be enjoyed on the ELR include Classes 20, 24, 31, 33, 35, 42, 45, 47 and 52 – together with three different types of DMU. *David Flitcroft/PDS*

SUMMERSEAT was one of the smaller stations on the line from Bury to Rawtenstall. Perched above the River Irwell, it was built to serve a scattering of mills and millworkers' houses. The southbound platform is pictured from a passing train on 23 April 1954.

The goods yard closed in 1964 as the mills switched to road transport or closed altogether. The passenger service to Rawtenstall lasted until 1972, latterly with 'paytrain' operation in an attempt to cut costs, but it was to be another eight years before the line closed completely. The East Lancashire Railway Preservation Society then secured the preservation of the line, with considerable help from Greater Manchester County Council, Bury Metropolitan Council and Rossendale Borough Council. Trains began running again from Bury to Ramsbottom in 1987 and to Rawtenstall in 1991. The line is now one of the most thriving preserved railways in the country, carrying an average of 120,000 passengers a year. The re-opened Summerseat station is pictured on 15 March 2003, with a steam-hauled train setting off on the final stage of its journey to Bury. *H. C. Casserley/PDS*

HOLCOMBE BROOK: The 3½-mile branch to Holcombe Brook, opened in 1881, was the object of two early electrification schemes. The first was the experimental Dick-Kerr 3,500-volt DC overhead system, inaugurated in 1913. This was superseded just five years later by the 1,200-volt DC third-rail system, the same as had been adopted between Manchester and Bury. This system operated successfully for several decades, but when faced with the prospect of costly renewal in the early 1950s British Railways decided instead to replace the electric units with steam. The 'new' service is pictured at Holcombe Brook on 24 April 1951, with a push-pull train about to form the 3.00pm departure to Bury. The leading carriage is 24453, a Brake 3rd with driving compartment built in 1949. Coupled behind it is saloon 3461, built by the L&YR in 1907. The locomotive is Class 2P 2-4-2T No 50829.

The steam-operated passenger service to Holcombe Brook lasted just 14 months, while the branch terminus remained open for goods until 1960. The station area was then sold off for development, including a small shopping centre and adjacent car park, as pictured on 15 March 2003. *H. C. Casserley/PDS*

BRADLEY FOLD: Lying roughly halfway between Bury and Bolton, Bradley Fold was served by trains on the once important through route between Bolton and Rochdale. A curve also left this line just east of Bradley Fold, providing a connection with Radcliffe on the Manchester to Bury line. This turn-of-the-20th-century postcard shows Bradley Fold in L&YR days, looking towards Bolton, with lower-quadrant signals guarding the crossing.

The Radcliffe connection was closed to passengers in 1953 and completely in 1964. The remaining east-west route through Bradley Fold survived until the Bolton-Rochdale service was withdrawn in 1970. Then came the prospect of revival, as the 'Picc-Vic' electrification scheme would have seen Manchester-Bolton trains running over re-instated tracks via Radcliffe and Bradley Fold. However, that scheme never came to fruition, and various encroachments on the trackbed would now preclude any future re-opening. Instead, part of the trackbed forms a pleasant footpath, pictured on 15 March 2003. *John Ryan collection/PDS*

Bolton

BOLTON GREAT MOOR STREET: The first railway to reach Bolton was the 10-mile branch from Kenyon Junction on the original Liverpool to Manchester line. Passenger services between Kenyon Junction and a terminus at Bolton Great Moor Street began as early as 1831, within a year of the historic Liverpool-Manchester launch. The branch soon became part of the LNWR, which replaced the original Great Moor Street station with a second, larger, four-platform terminus in 1875. A separate line via Little Hulton provided the LNWR with a more direct link between Great Moor Street and Manchester, competing directly with the L&YR line through Farnworth.

Our 'past' photograph shows Great Moor Street in its later years, with Class 2 2-6-2T No 41215 departing with the 5.05pm service to Kenyon Junction on 24 April 1951.

Regular passenger services were withdrawn from Great Moor Street in 1954, though the station continued to see 'Wakes Weeks' specials for five further seasons. The raised station area was levelled and has since been made into a supermarket car park, as pictured on 17 February 2003. The clock tower provides a common point of reference with the 'past' picture. *H. C. Casserley/PDS*

FLETCHER STREET JUNCTION, BOLTON: Although the LNWR and L&YR became amalgamated as early as 1921, there was sufficient traffic to keep both companies' lines to Bolton open until the 1950s. The last train to use the LNWR Great Moor Street terminus, an RCTS special headed by Class 4 2-6-4T No 42289, stands beside Fletcher Street Junction box on 4 April 1959. Fletcher Street Junction lay just outside Great Moor Street and marked the divergence of the lines to Kenyon Junction and Manchester via Little Hulton.

Although parts of the Bolton to Kenyon Junction line are still clearly visible today, the site of Fletcher Street Junction has disappeared under a mound of rubble and earth, now covered with several decades of tree growth. The 'present' picture is dated 15 March 2003. *Gavin Morrison/PDS*

BOLTON (L&YR) SHED lay on the west side of the Manchester line, about three-quarters of a mile south of Bolton Trinity Street station. It retained a sizeable allocation of mainly freight engines throughout the LMS era and stayed open right up to the final year of steam in 1968. It was coded 26C until 1963 and 9K from then until closure. This atmospheric scene was captured on film on 6 June 1968, just weeks before the end. Locomotives on shed on that date included 'Black Fives' Nos 44947, 45073, 45290 and 45318, and 8Fs 48337 and 48773. Although the photograph also shows a Type 2 diesel interloper, the shed never had an allocation of main-line diesels.

The site of the shed remained derelict for nearly two decades and was then redeveloped as a housing estate, as pictured on 17 February 2003. *Roger Siviter/ PDS*

BOLTON EAST (1): The surviving L&YR lines through Bolton retained a fine selection of semaphore signals until the 1980s. Class 47 No 47223 passes signals controlled from Bolton East box as it approaches the station with 6M32, the 0330 from Lindsey refinery to Preston Docks, on 25 April 1984. In the distance can be seen the signal gantry at Burnden Junction, formerly controlling the south end of the Burnden triangle.

The much simplified track layout is pictured on 15 March 2003, with a newly introduced Virgin 'Voyager' unit forming the 0651 service from Birmingham New Street to Edinburgh. At the time of writing no scheduled freight traffic is routed via Bolton. Although the oil traffic to Preston Docks is expected to resume imminently after a gap of eight years, for pathing reasons the trains will be routed via either Blackburn or Chat Moss instead of via Bolton.

The third picture shows de-signalling in progress at Bolton East on 8 December 1985. *All PDS*

BOLTON EAST (2): The east (geographically south) end of Bolton Trinity Street station retained many traditional railway features into the 1980s, not least of which was the impressive goods warehouse that took over from Bolton Halliwell goods depot in 1981. Approaching Bolton East box on 13 August 1983 is Class 45 'Peak' No 45019, hauling the 1325 holiday train from Blackpool North to York. Within a few years trains such as this would become a rarity as the railway shifted towards unit-train operation. Just below the skyline are the imposing station buildings completed by the L&YR in 1904.

A much leaner but duller scene has resulted from the track remodelling, resignalling and station rebuilding schemes of the 1980s. The goods warehouse has gone too – one wonders if it might have become a listed building had it lasted longer. Even the parcels sidings on the left are now disused following the withdrawal of Royal Mail traffic in the 1990s. Perhaps the only enhanced feature compared with the 'past' picture is the repainted road bridge spanning the south end of the station. 'Pacer' unit No 142037 departs with the 1430 Wigan Wallgate to Shaw & Crompton service on 17 February 2003. *Both PDS*

BOLTON WEST: The first L&YR station at Bolton (Trinity Street) was opened in 1838, but soon became inadequate for the needs of a growing industrial town, and a new, larger station was completed in 1903. The L&YR took the opportunity to resignal the station area, commissioning a new box at Bolton West with a miniature-lever electro-pneumatic power frame. This was one of the earliest examples of power-operated points and signals in the country, and survived until the major Manchester North resignalling scheme of the 1980s. A Cravens 'power twin' diesel unit, Nos M50389 and M50793, takes the Blackburn line with a local train from Manchester Victoria on 23 September 1981.

The resignalling scheme of 1985 involved remodelling the station track layout completely, with bi-directional operation allowing the removal of the two diamond crossings at the west end; the right-hand track, serving the outer face of Bolton's island platform, is now the normal route for trains both to and from Blackburn. Class 150 unit No 150207 recedes with the 1400 Manchester Victoria to Clitheroe service on 17 February 2003. *Both PDS*

BROMLEY CROSS: The Bolton to Blackburn line was always considered a secondary route, and its ruling gradient of 1 in 72 at the Bolton end made it unsuitable for heavy freight traffic. In the 1960s the section from Bromley Cross to Blackburn was singled, with a passing loop at Darwen, and in the 1980s the first mile of the route from Bolton to the site of Astley Bridge Junction was also singled, leaving a 2-mile double-track section from Astley Bridge Junction to Bromley Cross. Class 104 DMU cars M50500 and M50444 pass the signal box – an East Lancashire Railway relic dating back to 1875 – with the 1714 Blackburn to Manchester Victoria service on 4 June 1983.

Twenty years later little has changed other than the replacement of the semaphores by colour light signals controlled from Manchester North signalling centre. Curiously, the signal box survives, as does – despite increasingly stringent safety regulations – the public foot crossing at the north end of the platforms. Unit 150149 calls with the 1339 service from Clitheroe to Manchester Victoria on 15 March 2003. *Both PDS*

ENTWISTLE: Looking at the remoteness of Entwistle on the map, it is hard to imagine the station there being as busy as it appears to have been in this postcard view from the early 20th century. The overhead signal box seems to straddle two through goods lines, with an island platform serving the adjacent passenger lines.

The goods yard was closed in 1959, several years before the publication of the Beeching Report. The station lived on as a passenger-only location – something of a rarity in the early 1960s – but was reduced to an unstaffed halt in 1971. Dense undergrowth now makes it difficult to take an exact equivalent of the 'past' photograph, but this view of 15 March 2003 shows the remaining single platform from ground level. In fine weather a popular pub causes severe road congestion on the narrow lane leading to the station, while the train service itself is little used, with many trains booked to run non-stop between Bromley Cross and Darwen. *John Ryan collection/PDS*

LOSTOCK JUNCTION: The first station at Lostock Junction had four platforms – two on the Preston line and two on the line to Wigan. It is pictured on 27 April 1965, nearly two years after the closure of the adjacent goods yard but with passenger trains still booked to call.

Complete closure in 1966 was followed by the swift removal of the platforms. The second picture, dated 11 June 1975, shows No 50040 passing the junction with a Manchester Victoria to Carlisle service. The armless signal posts on the gantry beyond the box show that the down slow line from Bolton to Lostock Junction has recently been taken out of use.

Housing development in the surrounding area prompted the opening of a new station in 1988, initially named Lostock Parkway to attract car users; platforms were provided on the Preston line only. 'Coradia' unit No 175105 calls with the 1352 service from Blackpool North to Manchester Airport on 15 March 2003. *H. C. Casserley/JCH/PDS*

BLACKROD: The Horwich branch was home to the last surviving L&YR railmotor, No 10617. It is pictured on the north-facing curve approaching Blackrod, where passengers could connect with trains to Manchester and Preston. The L&YR built a total of 18 railmotors between 1906 and 1911, and this last survivor was not withdrawn until 1948.

The Horwich branch retained its double-track formation well after its closure to passengers. With the M61 motorway now passing prominently over the railway, Class 25 No 7652 approaches Blackrod on 7 June 1972 with an unusually long rake of wagons from Horwich Works. The scene pre-dates the BR TOPS renumbering scheme – this particular locomotive was soon to become No 25302 – and provides an example of the four-character headcodes displayed by most diesels and electrics until the mid-1970s. The '9' denoted an unfitted freight and the 'J' denoted the North Manchester area.

The Horwich branch saw its last revenue-earning train in September 1989 and most of the track was removed by 1992. Proposals to re-open the branch for domestic waste traffic came to nothing and the trackbed is slowly returning to nature, as pictured on **15 March 2003.** *John F. Ward collection/Tom Heavyside/PDS*

HORWICH WORKS: The town of Horwich owes much of its importance to the L&YR engine works built there in the 1880s. Occupying part of a 360-acre green-field site, the works was almost entirely self-contained, with its own facilities for boiler-making and foundry work. From 1889 until 1963 it turned out 1,830 steam locomotives, five narrow-gauge locomotives and 169 diesel shunters. Thereafter it concentrated on repairing wagons and electric multiple units. The works had its own extensive network of sidings, including some 7½ miles of 1ft 6in-gauge track. Our 'past' photograph shows *Wren*, one of eight similar 1ft 6in-gauge locos built for the works, resting between duties on 19 May 1935.

The 1960s marked the start of a long period of decline, as the various functions of the works were transferred elsewhere. In 1988 British Rail Engineering Limited sold the remaining facilities to Parkfield Foundries and the days of the town's railway connections were all but finished. However, most of the works buildings survived and have recently been incorporated into an industrial estate, as seen on 15 March 2003.

The railway origins of the industrial estate are kept alive by its name – Horwich Loco – as well as by a fine selection of railway artefacts and pictures in the main office block. This striking sign stands at the estate entrance.
John F. Ward collection/PDS (2)

HORWICH STATION: The 1½-mile branch to Horwich was opened by the L&YR in 1870, some 27 years after the opening of the main line from Bolton to Preston. Its single passenger platform handled through trains to and from Manchester as well as the local shuttle to and from Blackrod. Our 'past' picture dated 4 April 1959 depicts a scene that appears to have changed little since the days of the L&YR.

Public passenger services were withdrawn from Horwich in 1965, and goods facilities in the following year. The station area was converted into a public open space, as shown in the 'present' photograph of 15 March 2003. The cobbled ramp that led down to the platform is still discernible. The name Horwich returned to the railway timetable in 1999 when BR opened Horwich Parkway station on the nearby main line – almost a return to the pre-1870 situation when the station now called Blackrod was known as Horwich Road. *Gavin Morrison/PDS*

Wigan

ATHERTON: The L&YR opened its direct line from Manchester to Wigan via Atherton in 1888. As well as attracting new commuters from the suburbs to central Manchester, the line provided the L&YR with a quicker route for its Manchester-Liverpool expresses, previously routed via Bolton. The company even installed water troughs at Walkden, the next station east of Atherton. The decline of the line began in the 1950s with the closure of two small intermediate halts. During the 1960s the various station goods yards were closed and the line was reduced from quadruple to double track. By the 1980s all that remained was a basically hourly local passenger service, illustrated by this two-car Class 104 unit, Nos M53437 and M53480, heading for Manchester on 5 September 1983.

Threats of closure were averted and the Atherton line has survived into the 21st century. A visit on 15 March 2003 found a revised track layout using the central island platform, but still under the control of semaphore signals. Class 142 unit No 142004, one of the first batches of 'Pacers' built in 1985, forms the 0716 service from Kirkby to Manchester Victoria. *Both PDS*

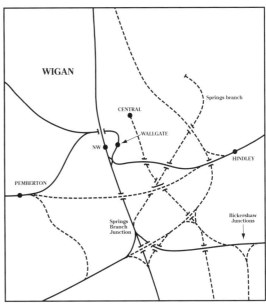

TYLDESLEY: An intricate network of lines and sidings once served the coal-mining area to the west and south of Wigan, and some duplication arose because the L&YR and the LNWR were essentially competing for the same business. The station at Tyldesley, illustrated here in pre-Grouping days, lay on the LNWR direct line from Manchester to Wigan, running parallel to and barely a mile away from the L&YR line via Atherton. Tyldesley was also the junction for trains to Leigh and Kenyon Junction, not to mention the freight-only links to Bickershaw (via Leigh) and Chequerbent (via a spur at Howe Bridge).

The Tyldesley line was nominated for closure in the Beeching Report. The service from Manchester to Wigan via Tyldesley was withdrawn in 1964. Strong local resistance brought a temporary reprieve for the Leigh line, but this too succumbed to the axe in 1969. Since then there has been talk of re-opening the railway or converting it to a busway, but for the moment nature is firmly in control, as seen on 15 March 2003. *John Ryan collection/PDS*

BICKERSHAW (1): The origins of Bickershaw Colliery go right back to the late 1830s, when pits operated by the Turner Ackers Company were connected by means of a tramway to the Leeds & Liverpool Canal. The colliery soon gained main-line railway connections, with the LNWR opening a link from Wigan to Leigh via Bickershaw and the GCR building a connection from its Wigan Central branch. This view, dated about 1908 and looking north from the canal side, shows a fine selection of wooden-bodied wagons awaiting loading or dispatch.

The railway sidings beside the canal were abandoned long ago, although the colliery still had working steam as late as 1983. The 'present' picture of 15 March 2003 shows the derelict site of the once bustling sidings, with only the traces of a former canal bridge enabling positive identification of the site. *John Ryan collection/PDS*

BICKERSHAW (2): During the miners' strike of 1984/85 the once intricate layout of sidings at Bickershaw was reduced to the bare minimum of one line under the rapid-loading bunker, together with a short cripple siding. The absence of a run-round loop meant that trains operated in 'top and tail' mode on the 5-mile branch between Wigan and Bickershaw, initially using two pairs of Class 20s and later two Class 60s. Pushing their train under the bunker on 7 June 1989 are Nos 20045 and 20159, while out of sight at the other end of the train are sister locomotives 20143 and 20130. At this time Bickershaw and Parkside were the last two rail-connected collieries in the North West, both supplying Fidlers Ferry power station.

The closure announcement for Bickershaw came in January 1992 and the colliery wound its last coal in March of that year. The final loaded train left the branch on 21 May. The site has since been levelled, and the only definite link with the 'present' picture of 13 May 2003 is the mound of ash beside the embankment in the bottom left-hand corner. Parkside Colliery lasted a few months longer than Bickershaw, closing in October 1992. *Both PDS*

BICKERSHAW (3): The GCR Wigan branch was a comparatively late addition to the Lancashire railway network, opening in stages between 1879 and 1884. It was first promoted by the CLC, with the principal aim of carrying coal from Bickershaw and other pits in the area. However, the Midland Railway – one of the constituents of the CLC – withdrew at an early stage and the line was operated independently until its absorption by the GCR in 1906. In British Railways days it was a little-known backwater, although it handled through trains between Wigan and Manchester right to the end. Ex-LMS Class 2 2-6-0 No 46448 approaches Bickershaw station with a southbound train in May 1956.

The passenger service between Glazebrook and Wigan was withdrawn in November 1964. The duplication of routes in the area enabled British Railways to transfer its goods traffic to other lines, and the trackbed was largely handed over to nature. Our 'present' photograph, dated 15 March 2003, shows the site of the former level crossing, with a line of trees hinting at the abandoned route. *C. H. Townley/PDS*

GOLBORNE: Ex-LMS 'Black Five' 4-6-0 No 45258 races through Golborne on the West Coast main line with an up troop train on 16 June 1962. At this time more than 800 'Black Fives' remained in service, concentrated mainly on the London Midland Region and on ex-LMS lines in Scotland. But diesels were already established on West Coast Main Line expresses, with a growing number of English Electric Type 4s (later Class 40) allocated to Crewe North and Carlisle Upperby sheds.

More than four decades later, on 9 April 2003, a Virgin driving van trailer heads the 1230 Glasgow Central to London Euston service past the same spot. The bridge that once carried the GCR St Helens branch over the West Coast main line has long since been removed, although a short stretch of the St Helens branch remains in use for freight traffic, connected to the main line by a curve installed in 1967. *Ian Holt/PDS*

WIGAN SPRINGS BRANCH (1): The name Springs Branch refers to one of the oldest branch lines in the world, opened in 1838 to serve the coalfield on the south-east side of Wigan. When the LNWR built its engine shed at the branch junction, the name Springs Branch was applied to the shed. In the British Railways era, Springs Branch was home to a variety of mainly ex-LMS freight and mixed traffic locomotives. However, its allocation in the late 1950s and early 1960s also included a few ex-GCR Class 'J10' locomotives, some dating back to the 19th century. The last two survivors of that class, Nos 65157 and 65198, are pictured outside the shed on 25 June 1961. Both were withdrawn in August of that year.

Springs Branch shed closed to steam in 1967 but lived on as a diesel depot well into the BR era. It was still the day-to-day base for local freight locomotives until the 1990s, although by this time its maintenance functions had ceased. However, in 1999 Springs Branch attracted renewed interest when it became the location of EWS's national component recovery and disposal centre (CRDC), charged with the task of removing re-usable components from withdrawn locomotives. By early 2003 more than 60 locomotives had been processed at the CRDC, most finishing up as scrap but some being sold intact for further use. Nearest the camera on 18 February 2003 are Class 37 locos Nos 37074 and 37071, both having arrived at the CRDC in 2000 after working in France on the new high-speed line to Avignon. *John F. Ward/PDS*

WIGAN SPRINGS BRANCH (2): Pressure on the main line between Springs Branch and Wigan North Western was relieved by the opening of the Whelley loop between Ince Moss and Standish in 1882, but even so the original route remained busy and was eventually expanded to six running lines. English Electric Type 4 (later Class 40) No D298 approaches Springs Branch with the up Sunday 'Royal Scot' on 13 June 1965. By this time most passenger trains in the North West were diesel-hauled, and the Class 40s on trains such as this were soon to give way to the new build of more powerful Class 50s.

Electrification between Crewe and Preston was inaugurated in 1973. During the electrification project BR took the opportunity to remove redundant or under-used tracks, leaving just four running lines between Springs Branch and Wigan North Western. Today most trains use the fast lines, although with the increased speed differential between Virgin 'Pendolinos' and 60mph freight workings the slow lines may yet become busier again. Still comprising Mark III stock with a Class 90 locomotive bringing up the rear, the 1320 Preston to London Euston train heads south on 9 April 2003. *Michael Mensing/PDS*

WIGAN NORTH WESTERN station was rebuilt in 1888, replacing a smaller station of 1838 on the same site. It was the subject of an early power signalling scheme, as illustrated in this view dated 21 April 1951. 'Black Five' No 45449 of Springs Branch shed stands in one of the bay platforms with a southbound passenger train. On the right are some wagons in the station goods yard, including a six-wheeled former tender in LMS livery, converted to a sludge wagon for water-softening purposes. Out of sight behind the wagons are the running lines of the ex-L&YR approach to Wigan Wallgate, which was built alongside – and to connect with – the LNWR line at this point.

North Western station was remodelled as part of the 1970s electrification scheme. Rather ominously, a single bay platform was retained on the up side for future use by connecting trains to Manchester – the intention at that time being to close Wigan Wallgate station and the ex-LYR lines from Wigan to Southport and Liverpool. Fortunately that threat was not carried out, and the up bay at Wigan North Western now handles local trains to and from Liverpool via St Helens. Unit No 142012 departs with the 0930 service to Liverpool Lime Street on 18 February 2003. Wigan North Western remains an unusual example of a station named after a pre-Grouping railway company. *H. C. Casserley/PDS*

WIGAN CENTRAL: Wigan's long-forgotten terminal station was opened in 1892 as an extension of the independent branch from Glazebrook, acquired by the GCR in 1906. The original terminus of the branch, at Darlington Street, lived on as a goods station. The 'new' passenger station became known as Wigan Central; it is pictured here in British Railways days, with a rake of ex-LMS and ex-SR parcels stock in the bay platform. Although the ex-GCR branch had a self-contained passenger service, there were three connections in the Hindley area that allowed the transfer of goods traffic to and from the ex-LNWR network.

Wigan Central closed to passengers in 1964 and to goods in 1965. A search for the former station site on 18 February 2003 was aided by the street named Station Road, but the only hint of a railway at the location is a small level area now turned into a car park. *Lens of Sutton collection/PDS*

WIGAN WALLGATE (1): Like its LNWR neighbour, the L&YR station at Wigan Wallgate was rebuilt in the late 19th century. It was – and still is today – the busy intersection of lines to Bolton, Manchester (via Atherton), Southport and Liverpool (via Rainford). The station frontage is pictured on 16 September 1970, with a typical selection of 1960s cars waiting outside.

At street level Wallgate station has changed little in the last 30 or more years. A proposal has been made to provide a covered link between Wallgate and North Western stations, but this seems unlikely to happen in view of current financial constraints. The 'present' view is dated 18 February 2003. *H. C. Casserley/PDS*

WIGAN WALLGATE (2): The rebuilding scheme of 1896 gave Wallgate a single island platform with one bay at the west end. There were also goods avoiding lines on each side. Standing in the bay on 27 April 1965 is Ivatt Class 4 2-6-0 No 43019, with Wolverton-built inspection saloon No M999505. The station was still gas-lit but semaphore signals had given way to colour lights.

The 'present' photograph of 18 February 2003 shows 'Pacer' No 142045 arriving at the eastbound platform to form the 0858 departure to Shaw & Crompton. The goods avoiding lines have been removed, and though the track in the bay platform is still there, it shows no sign of recent use. The signals appear to be the same as in 1965.
H. C. Casserley/PDS

WHITE BEAR was one of two intermediate stations on the secondary line from Wigan to Chorley, opened in 1869 to provide a more direct route for coal traffic between the East Lancashire towns and Garston Docks. It linked LNWR and L&YR metals and was operated independently by the Lancashire Union Railway. The line carried little passenger traffic and one of its two stations, Red Rock, closed as early as 1949. White Bear survived until the withdrawal of the Wigan to Chorley service in 1960. After that, the line remained open for goods until the late 1960s. Class 5 4-6-0 No 45391 passes the disused station on 20 July 1966 with a southbound fitted freight.

The site of White Bear station has now been built over. However, the 'present' scene of 15 March 2003 shows an old stone building that formerly stood on the northbound platform – and part of which is just visible at the extreme left of the 'past' photograph. *Ian Holt/PDS*

COPPULL: Class 5 4-6-0 No 44790 heads north through Coppull with a mixed freight on 31 August 1963. Near the front of the train are some 'Palvan' wagons, a late 1950s variation of the time-honoured 12-ton van designed specifically for loading with wooden pallets.

The changes of the last 40 years give the modern scene of 9 April 2003 a completely different feel, even though some features such as the church tower and road overbridge are unchanged. The remaining double-track railway has been electrified and resignalled and is flanked by the now ubiquitous metal fencing. The graveyard is still there but surrounded by commercial development. A Class 221 'Voyager' unit speeds north with the 1113 Plymouth to Edinburgh service. *Ian Holt/PDS*

GATHURST: It was not unusual for station goods yards to live on in the 1970s and 1980s for specific traffic flows. A case in point was Gathurst, where a nearby commercial explosives works kept the yard in business until the mid-1980s. Class 25 No 25192 shunts air-braked vans while working the 6T72 trip working from Warrington on 29 August 1985. At that time all wagons carrying explosives had to be flanked by barrier vehicles – in this instance they are two redundant ferry vans, one next to the locomotive and the other waiting on the main line to be reattached to the rear of the train.

Traces of the headshunt and main-line connection remain today, more than 20 years after the yard closed. The station meanwhile remains open for passengers. A Class 150 and Class 142 pairing makes its call with an evening Manchester-Southport service on 9 April 2003. *Both PDS*

PEMBERTON: Traces of the two main industries of the Wigan area – coal-mining and textiles – are prominent on the skyline as BR Standard Class 4 4-6-0 No 75046 passes Pemberton Junction with the 5.45pm Liverpool Exchange to Bolton train on 13 June 1965. Running across the centre of the picture is the start of the Wigan avoiding line, which the L&YR opened in 1889 to provide a shorter and quicker route between Manchester and Liverpool.

The Wigan avoiding line closed in 1969 after British Railways had decided to concentrate its Manchester-Liverpool expresses on the ex-LNWR route. Indeed, the passenger timetable for 1967/68 shows all remaining trains between Manchester and Liverpool Exchange booked to call at Wigan Wallgate. Today, as pictured on 9 April 2003, it is hard to imagine that Pemberton was ever a junction. *Michael Mensing/PDS*

St Helens

ASHTON-IN-MAKERFIELD: A remnant of the former GCR St Helens branch remained in use to serve the Lowton Metals scrapyard at Ashton-in-Makerfield long after the branch closed to passengers in 1952. Class 20 loco Nos 20106 and 20041 prepare to depart from the disused Ashton-in-Makerfield station with the 6T72 trip working to Warrington Walton Old Junction yard on 3 April 1986, conveying two POA wagons with scrap for Stocksbridge. This sort of trip working was soon to become history as BR ran down its Speedlink wagonload network and transferred as much traffic as possible to block trains.

Up-market commercial premises now occupy the site of the scrapyard and station – what a contrast! The 'present' scene is dated 9 April 2003. *Both PDS*

HAYDOCK station, also on the GCR St Helens branch, is pictured looking towards St Helens on 26 April 1951, just under a year before the withdrawal of the branch passenger service. This was a different location from Haydock Park station, which was located west of Ashton-in-Makerfield and handled race specials until the 1970s.

Goods traffic on the GCR St Helens branch lingered until the mid-1960s, after which the section west of Ashton-in-Makerfield was abandoned. A short stretch was then re-instated to serve a Shell distribution depot just west of the old Haydock station, but this was closed by the early 1980s and the line was cut back to Ashton again. The row of terraced houses on the left of the 'past' picture still stands today, but, apart from a glimpse of the roofline, now devoid of chimney stacks, it is masked by a more recent housing development. The 'present' photograph is dated 9 April 2003. *H. C. Casserley/PDS*

ST HELENS JUNCTION: The decision taken by the Liverpool & Manchester Railway in the 1820s to follow a route avoiding St Helens by a margin of 2 miles made the town something of a railway backwater. Even after the opening of various lines serving central St Helens, the L&MR station, now known as St Helens Junction, remained the closest calling point to the town for most long-distance expresses. Approaching the station on 20 August 1984 is Class 47 No 47152 with the 0750 trans-Pennine train from Scarborough to Liverpool Lime Street. In the background are the exchange sidings for Bold Colliery, still producing rail traffic at that time.

The rail connection to Bold was officially taken out of use in 1989. Since then the sidings have become completely overgrown, the colliery has been demolished and even the 'mountains' of colliery waste have diminished in size. The line no longer sees locomotive-hauled passenger trains, although it has become busier in recent years with freight to and from Liverpool Docks. Class 66 No 66240 heads west with 4Z64, the 0555 Daventry to Seaforth intermodal train, on 10 April 2003. This was one of a number of new intermodal services introduced by EWS in 2003, operating in direct competition with Freightliner. *JCH/PDS*

SUTTON OAK (1): The LNWR introduced a number of railmotor or push-pull services in the St Helens district in the early years of the 20th century. The service between St Helens Shaw Street and Widnes lasted into British Railways days, with intermediate halts at Peasley Cross and Sutton Oak, located at the St Helens end. A third halt at Robins Lane had closed in 1938, less than two years after its opening. Still with its LMS livery and number, Class 1P 2-4-2T No 6628 calls at Sutton Oak with the 6.11pm Widnes to St Helens working on 26 April 1951. The coaches are ex-LNWR push-pull stock, Nos 3441 and 3418.

The local service between St Helens and Widnes was withdrawn just two months after the date of the 'past' photograph. The section of line between St Helens and St Helens Junction survived as a through route for passenger trains until 1965 and for freight until 1989. The track was then taken up south of St Helens Hays siding (formerly Leathers Chemicals). Recently there has been talk of re-opening the St Helens to St Helens Junction route to passengers, although – as with all such projects – the cost would be considerable. The vacant trackbed is pictured on 10 April 2003. *H. C. Casserley, courtesy John F. Ward/PDS*

SUTTON OAK (2): Sutton Oak shed was situated on the east side of the St Helens-Widnes line, between Peasley Cross and Sutton Oak halts. It was a single-ended brick-built shed with ten roads. Our 'past' photograph was taken in 1937, looking east with the double-track line to Widnes in the foreground.

   The shed remained in operation until the last full year of BR main-line steam, finally closing on 19 June 1967. In later years its allocation included a variety of ex-LMS freight engines as well as BR Standard Class 4MT 2-6-0 and Class 'WD' 2-8-0 types. After closure, the shed site lay derelict for many years before being converted into a supermarket. In 2002 the old structure was finally demolished to make way for an entirely new building – albeit with an uncanny railway feel to it. The 'present' scene is dated 10 April 2003. *John F. Ward collection/PDS*

RAVENHEAD: The town of St Helens has a glass-making heritage going back to the 18th century. The railways became heavily involved in moving raw materials, such as sand, and various types of finished product, such as plate-glass and fibreglass. By 1989 the only remaining traffic was heavy fuel oil, discharged at two terminals – Cowley Hill and Ravenhead. The flow to Ravenhead at that time used the northern end of the former St Helens-Widnes line to reach the discharge terminal. Recalling the brief era of Trainload Freight, Petroleum-liveried Class 47 No 47381 pulls the first half of its train of empty tanks out of the Ravenhead terminal on 15 February 1989. Once coupled to the other half, it will form the 1336 departure to Robeston refinery.

Rail-borne petroleum traffic declined sharply in the 1990s as many users switched to road deliveries – or to other sources of fuel. The original Ravenhead terminal was closed shortly after the date of the 'past' photograph to make way for a new road and retail development, as seen on 10 April 2003. But that is not the end of the story. Just visible on the extreme right of the newer photograph is a rake of oil wagons, awaiting discharge after arriving from Immingham. The road-building scheme included not only this replacement rail terminal, but also a new rail connection into the terminal from the St Helens to Huyton line, cutting out the need to use the rump of the St Helens Junction line. *Both PDS*

ST HELENS SHAW STREET: The LNWR opened its direct line between Huyton (Liverpool) and Wigan via St Helens in 1872. At last St Helens lay on a line connecting two major centres, and the LNWR provided the town with a much-enlarged station, later known as Shaw Street. The 'past' photograph shows the station on 27 April 1951, with the main line to Wigan on the left and the bay platform for the Widnes service on the right.

In 1961 the LNWR edifice was demolished to make way for new buildings – with a liberal use of locally manufactured glass! – which are still in use today. The station was renamed St Helens Central in May 1987, long enough after the closure of the original ex-GCR St Helens Central to avoid confusion. 'Pacer' units Nos 142052 and 142055 make their call with an early morning service for Liverpool on 10 April 2003. The 1961 station is now past its best and there are plans for a 21st-century replacement. *H. C. Casserley/PDS*

ST HELENS CENTRAL: The first station named St Helens Central was the terminus of the rather obscure GCR branch line from Lowton St Marys, seen earlier at Ashton-in-Makerfield and Haydock. Regular passenger services to St Helens Central did not begin until 1900, well after the rest of the railway network in the area was complete. The branch kept its pre-Grouping associations after Nationalisation; ex-GCR Class 'J10' 0-6-0 No 65189 arrives on 26 April 1951 with the 8.00am service from Manchester Central.

Given that the station closed over half a century ago, on 3 March 1952, it is not surprising that no trace of it remains today. Birchley Street car park now occupies the site, as pictured on 10 April 2003. *H. C. Casserley/PDS*

PRESCOT: In the 1980s BR still operated numerous local trip workings for wagonload traffic, often carrying just a handful of wagons and sometimes cancelled at short notice if there was no traffic on offer. The 'Target 75' trip working from Warrington conveyed traffic for various terminals in the St Helens area, including Leathers Chemicals (later Hays) at Ravenhead and BICC at Prescot. Class 25 No 25315 shunts the Prescot BICC sidings while working 'Target 75' on 27 April 1984; it has just deposited one ferry van for loading and will now return to St Helens with the tank wagon.

The private sidings at Prescot were officially closed in March 1990, regular traffic having ceased some time before this. However, the chemical traffic from Hays was to continue until 2002, surviving the end of the Speedlink wagonload network in 1991 because the receiving customer – Roche Products at Dalry – insisted on delivery by rail. The 'present' view of Prescot shows unit No 150224 passing the remnants of the BICC sidings while working the 0732 from Liverpool Lime Street to Blackpool North on 10 April 2003. *Both PDS*

Widnes and Warrington

WIDNES SOUTH station was located on a 1½-mile loop known as the Widnes Deviation, opened by the LNWR in 1869 to avoid an awkward level crossing on the original Widnes-Warrington line. The station is pictured on 10 April 1957, looking towards Warrington. Curving away to the right behind Widnes No 7 signal box is the spur to the Widnes-St Helens line.

Widnes South closed to passengers in 1962 but the line remains open for freight to this day, mainly coal traffic from Liverpool Docks to Fidlers Ferry power station. The spur to the St Helens line lost its passenger service in 1951 and closed completely in the 1980s. Part of the Widnes-St Helens trackbed has since been turned into the A557 trunk road. The modern scene, with the cooling towers of Fidlers Ferry on the skyline, was recorded on 2 March 2003. *H. C. Casserley/PDS*

WIDNES TANHOUSE LANE: The Blue Circle cement terminal at Tanhouse Lane had an unusually complex history. It was originally reached by a spur from the CLC Widnes Central loop, opened as a through route between Sankey and Hough Green in 1878. To allow the closure of this loop in 1961, British Railways provided a new curve into Tanhouse Lane sidings from the ex-LNWR Widnes-St Helens line. When that line in turn faced closure, BR provided another new connection to Tanhouse Lane, this time from the ex-LNWR Widnes Deviation. Shunting a mixture of air-braked and vacuum-braked cement wagons at Tanhouse Lane on 7 July 1983 is pilot loco No 08838.

Tanhouse Lane remained in use until 2000, when Blue Circle replaced it – and the company's Northenden railhead – with a new terminal at Weaste (see page 12). The 'present' photograph of January 2003 shows how quickly nature can take over. *Both PDS*

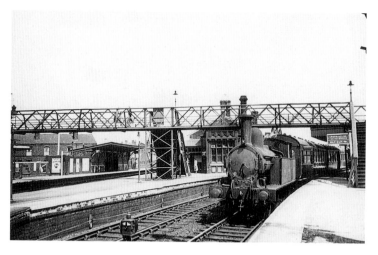

EARLESTOWN became a junction as early as 1831 when the Warrington & Newton Railway opened its branch from Earlestown on the original Liverpool & Manchester line. The station at Earlestown gained platforms on all three sides of the triangle. The first photograph shows a train from Warrington calling at the south-to-west platform around 1950, hauled by an ex-LNWR 2-4-2 tank engine. The building on the island platform dates from Liverpool & Manchester days.

The south-to-west curve lost its regular passenger service in 1965 but remained a significant route for freight. The second picture shows Class 40 No 40181 rounding the very tight curve with a Blodwel to St Helens ballast train on 21 February 1983. This train would have used the now-closed link between St Helens Junction and St Helens Shaw Street.

BR re-introduced a passenger service over the now singled south-to-west curve in May 1994. This included some through trains between Liverpool and Ellesmere Port via Warrington – a somewhat roundabout journey. 'Pacer' unit No 142039 forms the 1351 from Warrington Bank Quay to Liverpool Lime Street on 18 February 2003. *F. W. Shuttleworth, courtesy John F. Ward/PDS (2)*

KENYON JUNCTION was another very early railway junction, situated at the green-field site where the 1831 Leigh & Kenyon Junction Railway joined the Liverpool & Manchester line. The 'past' photograph, dated 23 August 1952, shows the Liverpool to Manchester line in the foreground and the branch to Leigh and Bolton curving left beyond the footbridge. The designers of the footbridge evidently imagined that this was to become a major interchange station; the reality is that it gradually became redundant as traffic shifted to other more conveniently routed lines.

The branch to Leigh and Bolton closed to passengers in 1954, while Kenyon Junction lasted until 1961 as an intermediate station on the Liverpool-Manchester line. The 'present' photograph was taken on 10 April 2003. *H. C. Casserley/PDS*

WINWICK JUNCTION (1): Originally trains between Warrington and Wigan were routed via a short stretch of the Liverpool & Manchester Railway between Earlestown and Lowton. The direct line between Winwick Junction and Golborne did not open until 1864. Even then, stopping trains on the West Coast Main Line continued to follow the old route until Lowton station closed in 1949. Negotiating the curve on the 'new' line at Winwick Junction on 29 August 1963 is 'Princess Coronation' or 'Duchess' 4-6-2 No 46225 *Duchess of Gloucester* with an up express. The 'Duchesses' were a powerful and successful design, and some examples remained on premier West Coast Main Line duties until withdrawal in 1964.

The track layout at Winwick Junction was remodelled as part of the early 1970s electrification scheme. Southbound trains from Earlestown now use the down fast line for a short distance before crossing over on to one of the up tracks. Four Class 86 locomotives, Nos 86430, 86607, 86639 and 86631, head the late-running 0500 Coatbridge to Crewe Freightliner service on 18 February 2003. *Hugh Ballantyne/PDS*

WINWICK JUNCTION (2): Stanier 8F 2-8-0 No 48307 approaches Winwick Junction with a down engineers' train on 28 August 1965. More than 700 8Fs were built from 1935 onwards and they became the mainstay of heavy freight services on many parts of the LMS system. No 48307 was, like many of the class, to remain in service until 1968.

Today the 1960s road overbridge at Winwick Junction is one of the few relatively uncluttered vantage points for photographing the West Coast Main Line. The four tracks between Warrington and Winwick Junction, reducing to three at the junction itself, are busy with passenger and freight traffic. Still carrying its obsolete Trainload Coal livery, Class 60 No 60057 *Adam Smith* takes the Earlestown line with 6F70, the 1633 coal empties from Fidlers Ferry to Liverpool Bulk Terminal, on 13 May 2003. The wagons are JMAs, originally owned by National Power but now transferred to EWS ownership. *Hugh Ballantyne/PDS*

WARRINGTON CENTRAL (1): The engine 'shed' on the CLC line at Warrington Central was in reality nothing more than a couple of sidings with an engine pit, squeezed into a narrow strip of land beside the passenger station. And yet it was to remain in use until 1966, outliving the shed at Liverpool Brunswick to which it was attached as a sub-shed. Recalling the days of GCR motive power on the Cheshire Lines, Class 'J10' 0-6-0 No 65166 is pictured at Warrington Central on 11 September 1955.

The high wall at Warrington Central now separates the Liverpool-bound platform from the A57 road, as pictured on 18 February 2003. The BR signal box in the distance was moved here from Platt Bridge Junction in the 1970s. *Bernard Mettam collection, courtesy John F. Ward/PDS*

WARRINGTON CENTRAL (2): The fine Cheshire Lines goods shed, displaying the names of the constituent railway companies, was already considered a historic monument when this photograph was taken on 25 April 1970. In the foreground are the yard pilot, Class 08 No D3578, and a 16-ton unfitted mineral wagon. Between them is what appears to be an unloading ramp for motor vehicles.

Today the preserved goods shed is well set back from the railway, the goods yard having finally closed in 1982 after a long period of decline. Loco D3578 became 08463 under the TOPS renumbering scheme and was withdrawn in 1989, although many of its classmates remain in service today. As for the 16-ton mineral wagon, the last examples of this once ubiquitous design – more than 250,000 of them were built – passed into history in the early 1980s. The 'present' photograph is dated 1 March 2003. *T. J. Edgington/PDS*

WARRINGTON DALLAM (1): This trio of photographs looking north from Dallam Branch Sidings shows three stages in the evolution of British rail freight. In the first picture, dated 24 August 1966, Class 9F 2-10-0 No 92156 heads south with a train of empty unfitted mineral wagons. The fan of sidings in the foreground gave access to various private sidings on the Dallam branch, which had been the original railway approach to Warrington from the north.

Considerable simplification has taken place by the date of the second photograph, 8 October 1990. Low-capacity unfitted wagons have given way to more efficient block train operation, with much general merchandise traffic now conveyed in containers. Class 86 No 86611 *Airey Neave* heads 4O81, the 0710 Freightliner service from Coatbridge to Southampton. The sidings in the foreground now give access only to Dallam freight terminal.

The third picture shows the slightly altered track layout installed in the 1990s to serve the Royal Mail distribution depot, visible on the right. Class 90 No 90021 departs with 1A90, the 1532 Warrington to Wembley mail train, on 20 May 2003. Unfortunately Royal Mail announced in June 2003 that it was to pull out of rail altogether, presaging a bleak future for the Warrington depot and seven similar purpose-built facilities in other parts of the country. Rail freight generally seems to be under much greater pressure today than it was even in 1990, with spiralling costs and ever-stronger road competition conspiring to stifle potential new traffic. *Tom Heavyside/PDS (2)*

WARRINGTON DALLAM (2): Rail freight cannot exist without terminals, and yet in the last 20 years many potentially valuable terminal sites have been lost to non-railway redevelopment. Fortunately, that fate has so far spared Warrington, where the modest fan of sidings at Dallam remains available for traffic as required. The first photograph was taken on 10 April 1990, when Dallam was the receiving point for steel from Allied Steel & Wire at Cardiff as well as international traffic via the Dunkerque-Dover train ferry. The pilot loco is No 08809. A siding connection had recently been installed in the large warehouse in the background, with the intention of bringing in trainloads of freight from Europe via the Channel Tunnel.

Dallam lost its wagonload traffic after the demise of Speedlink, but was then used briefly as a transhipment point for the ill-fated Charterail Piggyback trains. The steel traffic then restarted, as did a flow of lighting products from Bodmin, but these flows both ended by 2001. The terminal then saw a period of intensive use by a daily intermodal train to and from Glasgow Deanside. The second picture shows a 45-foot Deanside swapbody being loaded on 1 August 2001.

At the time of writing, no revenue-earning traffic is using Dallam freight depot, the Deanside traffic having ceased in early 2002. The converted FJA Freightliner flats seen in the third picture, dated 10 April 2003, had gone by May and the sidings were rusty again. But that is, we hope, not the end of the story. *All PDS*

WARRINGTON BANK QUAY (1): Awaiting the right of way from the down goods loop at Bank Quay station on 1 August 1967 is 'Black Five' 4-6-0 No 45133. A glance at the working timetable for that year shows that 23 freight trains were booked to pass Bank Quay in the down direction between 7.00am and 9.00pm on an average weekday, excluding 'specials' and local trip workings.

By today's standards, the West Coast Main Line remains a busy route for freight, though there are only about half the number of booked freight workings as in 1967. By contrast, the frequency of passenger trains has increased, especially since the new service to Liverpool via Earlestown started in 1994. 'Pacer' unit No 142009 forms the 1051 departure to Liverpool Lime Street on 10 April 2003. *Tom Heavyside/PDS*

WARRINGTON BANK QUAY (2): 'Britannia' Class 7P6F 4-6-2 No 70002 *Geoffrey Chaucer* enters Bank Quay station with an afternoon train from London Euston to Barrow on 21 June 1966; the 'Britannia' would have replaced an electric locomotive at Crewe. The train appears to be a complete rake of BR Mark I stock, with a GUV parcels van behind the locomotive. The south end of the station still has semaphore signals, controlled from Warrington No 1 box, which is just visible behind the train.

Nearly 37 years later, on 10 April 2003, Class 87 No 87006 *George Reynolds* arrives with the 1430 service from London Euston to Glasgow Central, passing EWS Class 92 No 92006 *Britten* in the up holding siding. Most Virgin West Coast services were then in the hands of Class 87 and 90 locomotives, with rakes of Mark III stock operating in fixed-formation push-pull mode. But not for much longer! The first of the replacement 'Pendolino' trains was already undergoing testing when this photograph was taken. *H. C. Casserley/PDS*

WARRINGTON BANK QUAY (3): The low-level station at Warrington Bank Quay had platforms at right angles to those on the West Coast Main Line. It was served by local trains on what now seems an unlikely route from Liverpool to Manchester via Ditton Junction and Timperley. Ex-LMS Class 2 2-6-2T No 41288 prepares to depart from Bank Quay Low Level with the 4.18pm to Manchester London Road on 24 March 1962. The skyline is dominated by the Lever Brothers factory, with the high-level platforms of the West Coast Main Line running across the middle of the picture.

The passenger service between Ditton Junction and Timperley was withdrawn in the autumn of 1962 and the low-level station was abandoned. However, the double-track line between Ditton Junction and Warrington Arpley remains busy with freight. Making a change from the usual procession of Fidlers Ferry coal trains is EWS Class 37 No 37684 *Peak National Park*, heading the 0850 intermodal train from Seaforth to Warrington Arpley on 17 May 2003. *Keith Smith/ PDS*

WARRINGTON ARPLEY: The main engine shed for Warrington was at Dallam, but until 1963 there was also a small sub-shed at Arpley, conveniently situated for the nearby marshalling yard. Pictured outside Arpley shed on 2 August 1958 is Class 8F 2-8-0 No 48429. Also recorded inside the shed on that date were Class 2 2-6-2T No 41210 and Class 3F 0-6-0T No 47603.

The sidings on the site of the shed became a diesel stabling point, which they remained until EWS provided new facilities next to the West Coast Main Line in the 1990s. Since then, the former locomotive sidings have been used to store wagons. A visit on 10 April 2003 found a rake of PFA wagons with containers, which, judging by the warning labels, were carrying or had recently carried hazardous waste. *Jim Peden, courtesy John F. Ward/PDS*

LATCHFORD: English Electric Type 4 (later Class 40) No D350 passes Latchford sidings with empty 'Carflat' wagons on 12 February 1966. The 3M08 headcode enables the train to be identified as the 10.15am from Wrenthorpe to Speke (Ford's Sidings), one of a number of Class 3 block automotive trains to and from Speke at that time.

The former Lymm line was truncated at Latchford in 1985. Both the former main line and the adjacent sidings now form run-round loops for Fidlers Ferry coal trains and other services using the 'low-level' route. Class 60 No 60099 has just completed its run-round manoeuvre with 7F81, the 1019 coal train from Liverpool Bulk Terminal to Fidlers Ferry, on 18 February 2003. *Ian Holt/PDS*

THELWALL: About half a mile west of Thelwall station Class 2 2-6-2T No 41230 ambles along with the 5.34pm stopping train from Stretford to Warrington Bank Quay Low Level on 19 September 1961. Bringing up the rear of the train appears to be a two-axle goods van, possibly conveying parcels or mail traffic. Attaching a van like this was regular practice on some secondary passenger services, even after the introduction of diesel multiple units.

Regular passenger services on the line lasted another year after the date of the 'past' photograph, although railtours continued to use it until its complete closure in the mid-1980s. Much of the route has since been converted into a pleasant-cycle track and footpath, as pictured on 10 April 2003. *Michael Mensing/PDS*

INDEX OF LOCATIONS

BIBLIOGRAPHY

ABC British Railways Locomotives, combined volumes: various years (Ian Allan)

ABC Railway Freight Operations by Paul Shannon (Ian Allan)

BR Steam Motive Power Depots: LMR by Paul Bolger (Ian Allan)

BR Track Diagrams: No 4 London Midland Region (Quail Map Co)

The Cheshire Lines Committee by Paul Bolger (Heyday Publishing)

Complete British Railway Maps & Gazetteer 1839-1981 by C. J. Wignall (OPC)

Directory of British Engine Sheds 2 by Roger Griffiths and Paul Smith (OPC)

Freight Only Yearbook Nos 1 and 2 by Michael Rhodes and Paul Shannon (Silver Link Publishing)

The Heyday of Steam around Manchester by Tom Heavyside (Ian Allan)

The Lancashire & Yorkshire Railway by Alan Earnshaw (Ian Allan)

Miles Platting to Diggle (via Ashton) (Challenger Publications)

A Pictorial Survey of Railway Signalling by D. Allen and C. J. Woolstenholmes (OPC)

Railways in and around Manchester Suburbs by E. M. Johnson (Foxline)

A Regional History of the Railways of Great Britain: Volume 10 The North West by Geoffrey O. Holt (David & Charles)

Regional Railway Centres: North West by Rex Christiansen (Ian Allan)

Steam Motive Power Depots: Volume 3 by Paul Smith (Platform Five Publishing)

Back issues of:
Branch Line News
British Railways Illustrated
Modern Railways
Rail
Railway Magazine
The Railway Observer
Railway World